"If you haven't met Sara Olson-Smith, you will on these pages. She's as warm and compelling in print as she is in person—a truly gifted pastor, full of grace, integrity, and an unmistakable love for people."

—PETER W. MARTY, Editor and Publisher, *The Christian Century*

"Sara Olson-Smith bequeaths a faithful and beloved congregation's treasury of comfort, courage, and hope to every pastor, leader, and congregant facing the reality that their faith community can no longer be a church the way the church is meant to be. Beautiful vignettes interwoven with Scripture touch the heart, move to tears, and inspire conversation that empowers discerning with faith that trusts the promise of the Gospel. Congregations should read this book together!"

—CRAIG ALAN SATTERLEE, Theologian and Author

"The best eulogies tell the truth about the person who died, honoring the complexity of being human. Olson-Smith gives the best kind of eulogy in this book, not only in her truth telling, but in the ways she helps us see churches we have loved in all their complexity. This book is a must-read for clergy as we navigate the painful work of knowing when ministry is coming to an end, while helping a church to close with faithful courage."

—BROOKE PETERSEN, John H. Tietjen Chair of Pastoral Ministry, Lutheran School of Theology At Chicago

"*Eulogy for a Dying Church* offers heartwarming and heartbreaking testimony to the reality of grief, the persistence of faith, and an abiding trust that God is faithful to the promise of resurrected life. Most of all, it is a story of love. A must-read for all who wonder whether a lasting legacy remains when a congregation comes to the end of its life. The answer is a resounding yes!"

—Audrey West, Project Administrator, Thriving in Ministry: Moravian Clergy Connections

"With so much shifting underfoot, congregations often cling to life as they once knew it. Sara Olson-Smith offers a more Jesus-shaped way in this tender memoir. This is a beautiful story of everyday, faithful people who once met in a brick building in New Jersey. Weaving together stories from scripture and from kitchen tables, Olson-Smith finally weaves us all into a grieving, trusting, and hopeful people called Church."

—Jason A. Mahn, author of *Neighbor Love through Fearful Days*

Eulogy for a Faithful Church

Eulogy for a Faithful Church

The Story of a Congregation's Courageous Ending and Enduring Legacy

SARA OLSON-SMITH

RESOURCE *Publications* · Eugene, Oregon

EULOGY FOR A FAITHFUL CHURCH
The Story of a Congregation's Courageous Ending and Enduring Legacy

Copyright © 2026 Sara Olson-Smith. All rights reserved. Except for brief quotations in critical publications or reviews, no part of this book may be reproduced in any manner without prior written permission from the publisher. Write: Permissions, Wipf and Stock Publishers, 199 W. 8th Ave., Suite 3, Eugene, OR 97401.

Resource Publications
An Imprint of Wipf and Stock Publishers
199 W. 8th Ave., Suite 3
Eugene, OR 97401

www.wipfandstock.com

PAPERBACK ISBN: 979-8-3852-2848-5
HARDCOVER ISBN: 979-8-3852-2849-2
EBOOK ISBN: 979-8-3852-2850-8

VERSION NUMBER 03/16/26

"Dropping Keys" from *The Gift: Poems Inspired by Hafiz*, Daniel Ladinsky © 1999 with permission. www.danielladinsky.com.

Liturgical quotations from Evangelical Lutheran Worship. Copyright © 2024 Augsburg Fortress. All rights reserved. Used by permission.

Scripture quotations are taken from the New Revised Standard Version Updated Edition. Copyright © 2021 National Council of Churches of Christ in the United States of America. Used by permission. All rights reserved worldwide.

"The Poet Thinks About the Doney" by Mary Oliver. Reprinted by the permission of The Charlotte Sheedy Literary Agency as agent for the author. Copyright © 2006, 2017 by Mary Oliver with permission of Bill Reichblum.

We Are the Church, Words: Richard K. Avery & Donald Marsh © 1972 Hope Publishing Company, www.hopepublishing.com. All rights reserved. Used by Permission.

For all the saints of St. Peter's Lutheran Church

Contents

Acknowledgments

My deepest gratitude goes to the people of St. Peter's Lutheran Church. They taught me the complex beauty of congregational life and modeled a deep, lived faith. There may have only been a few dozen of them, but they have an outsized place in my heart. I can only hope that I have shared their story in a way that honors their faithfulness with honesty and love. I am particularly grateful for the ones known as Katherine, Clara, Debbie, Jill, and Nancy. For the conversations over Zoom, at the diner, among cacti, and at the beach, I am grateful.

Thank you to the people of Saints Basilios-Gregorios Orthodox Church in North Plainfield, especially Pastor Vijay Thomas and Mr. P.K. Jacob, for your hospitality and openness to sharing your building, your congregation, and your faith with me. Huge thanks also to Karen Anderson of EPES, Daniel Rift of Lutheran World Hunger, and staff at United Lutheran Seminary for helping me follow the generosity of St. Peter's to the people and stories. Thank you, Pastor Ashrouf Tannous, for the conversation, and for your faithful leadership as you continue to call the global church to deeper faithfulness, solidarity, and advocacy with our Palestinian siblings.

Thank you to the many people throughout New Jersey who supported me and cared for our congregation in the years of our discernment and since our closing. The two things I miss most about New Jersey are the bagels and my pastor colleagues in the New Jersey Synod of the Evangelical Lutheran Church in America.

Particular thanks to Bishop Roy E. Riley and Bishop Tracie Bartholomew for their encouragement and leadership, and to the staff in the office of the Bishop during my tenure in New Jersey. Many thanks to the people of St. Stephen's Lutheran Church in South Plainfield for offering a life raft to so many St. Peter's people and many more. Thanks to the people of Christ the King Lutheran Church in Kendall Park, now Abiding Love, for helping me find my feet again as a pastor.

I am grateful for the people of St. Paul Lutheran Church in Davenport, Iowa. Not only is this congregation a bright light of generosity, creativity, and service, but they're just an utter delight to be around. Thank you for the time away to write and travel in the summer of 2023 and for nurturing me as a writer. All the times you asked, "How's the book going?" kept me going through this long process.

There's a whiteboard inside the office door at St. Paul, which lists the staff and those magnetic dots noting if we are "in" or "out." Imagine that list here and know that each of those 20-some people (and each one listed there over the years) has contributed to this book in one way or another. An absent-minded, creative-type is not always the easiest of colleagues to work with, and your grace, encouragement, laughter, and above all, love of people (including me) has been the most profound gift. Particular thanks go to those who have carried a heavy load in both ministry and support of me: Peter, Katy, Peter, Mark, Chris, and Joel.

Thank you to Elizabeth Hunter at Gather Magazine for providing opportunities to write Bible Studies over the years and helping me gain confidence as a writer. And thank you to the people at Wipf and Stock who took a risk on a first-time author.

I am grateful to Leslie, Elaine (aka MOM), and Brooke for being first readers of early drafts. And for Karen, for reading these words so thoughtfully as I finished. Your feedback helped shape this book and kept me going when I felt overwhelmed.

Sarah, thank you for your thoughtful edits and for encouraging me (and countless others) as a writer. Mostly, I'm grateful for 30 years of friendship.

Peter, thank you for your careful, playful, and honest editing of this manuscript. You are beloved and dear to me. I am grateful for the ways you have helped to unlock a pastoral life that has been full of such joy. Serving with you and calling you a friend has been such a privilege. Thank you.

None of this could have happened without some places in this country which gave me space to think, to write, to imagine. I thank God for the quiet and beauty of Lake Sagatagan, Lake Chippewa, Lake Superior, Lake Michigan, and the Wet Mountain Valley of southern Colorado. (And for the College of St. Benedict/St. John's University, Rainbow Trail Lutheran

Camp, the Barry Olson Family, and the state parks of Wisconsin for sharing and protecting those sacred places.)

For dear friends who have stuck with me over the years. I'm grateful for you. LUSH, PWOW, the Bond Girls, the Camping Family, Beth&Leslie, and all those amazing friends and family who have walked alongside me along the way. I'm also so grateful for the communities of faith that have formed me. In the Denver area: Valley, Bethany and Holy Trinity, Zion in Wisconsin, and Hope in Eau Claire. I've had tremendous mentors and friends in Dave Jarvis at Rainbow Trail, Kelly Chatman at Redeemer in Minneapolis, everyone at LSTC, and John Calhoun at the Moscow Protestant Chaplaincy.

Audrey and Frank—thank you for the pizza and brownies. Conversations with you over the years have been the seeds that grew into this book. Audrey, you are one of the many strong and beautiful women of faith who have kept me going in ministry. Without your presence, I would have given up long ago. Thank you.

Red and Susan, you have nurtured and sustained my faith and call by your presence in my life and the testimony of your generosity and steadfast commitment to justice. Thank you for carrying on the stories of my Dad and for your humor, songs, and love.

Of course, it'd be impossible without my family. Brent and Connie, your endurance is found not just on bicycles but in the way you stick with people. I'm grateful to call you immediate family, and for the ways you bring more fun into my life and this world. Terry, thanks for your questions and for listening. MOM, you are my first and favorite cheerleader. Thank you for nurturing me in faith, creativity, and joy.

Susannah and Amos, there have been too many times when I've been distracted by ideas and buried in words, making me late for pick-up or burning dinner. You have been gracious and patient, and you bring me such joy. What remarkable humans you are. As much as I love being a pastor, Mama is still my favorite name.

Clark, I couldn't ask for a better partner. Thank you for being there the morning after, every day.

Lastly, I am grateful for my Dad, who gave me stories, the best gift anyone could receive.

Introduction

Every year I light a candle for them.

The flame of their votive dances alongside others, lined up like a choir. The small flames shine on All Saints' Day, when Christians remember and give thanks for God's beloved ones who have died. In the act of candle lighting, we reignite our trust in the resurrection. Death is not the end of the story. New life comes. The very worst thing is never the last thing.

In bold defiance against the powers of death, we light candles. In my Lutheran Christian tradition, each remembered person is named a saint, made holy by God's grace. They're not famous or miracle workers; they're simply people who have left an impact on our lives. Though I'm only midway through this life with twenty years of pastoral ministry under my belt, given enough votives, I could line up enough saint-inspired candles to land an airplane at night. It's not just the family and dear friends whose deaths have made permanent holes in my heart, but also now sainted parishioners who I've loved and buried.

A pastor's life is made up of goodbyes. We're invited into holy moments at the end of life. Silent hours passed in hospice rooms or loud, traumatic minutes in emergency rooms. We accompany people and their loved ones through heartbreaking goodbyes, bearing witness to hope. Nothing, not even the grave, can separate us from the love of Christ. In showing up, pastors embody the promise of God's presence through the valleys of the shadow of death.

Every All Saints' Day, I take time to remember those individuals whose living and dying have shaped me into the pastor and person I am. But each year, I light candles not just for individuals, but for a congregation, a congregation that is no longer. That candle burns in memory of a community of people who I had the honor of accompanying through their last years. This church ended its ministry just as I was beginning mine.

In the summer of 2006, with creases from the packaging still noticeable on my new clergy shirts and the ink on my seminary diploma still drying, I drove up to a small brick church in the central New Jersey township of North Plainfield. I was 28 years old and ready to begin the work for which I had spent years training. Expectations filled my heart as completely as the trunk of my tiny Toyota was packed with books. I couldn't wait to begin this vocation to which I had been called.

St. Peter's Lutheran Church took a big risk on me. They chose to use their precious and limited resources to pay for a full-time pastor, and not just any pastor—a young and idealistic woman from the Midwest. Even more miraculously, they entrusted me with their worries and hopes, spoken aloud in Bible studies and whispered in nursing homes, voices shaking with anger or sorrow in congregational meetings. The people of St. Peter's were the first ones to ever call me "Pastor." Their trust, care, and sometimes opposition gave me the confidence to claim this role.

Members of that congregation hoped I could change the trajectory of shrinking membership and steady decline. I thought it was possible, too, though I knew it would take all of us to do it. We tried all kinds of things. We had many brilliant ideas. Some were embraced and didn't work. Others were refused and never tried. Near the end of my second year at St. Peter's, it became clear that our current ways of doing ministry were unsustainable.

Sociologists, leadership coaches, and theologians have spilled plenty of ink about the decline of mainline Protestantism in the United States. The story of St. Peter's fits into those narratives. The combination of changing neighborhoods, shifting demographics, congregational conflict, institutional distrust, and significant social changes, among other factors, led to our decline. The people of St. Peter's and I spent enough time attempting to change realities that were beyond our control and bearing the weight of regret and sadness over what we could not do. The point of this book is not to examine every detail that led to our ending but instead to share how this congregation faced that reality and claimed a new future.

This book is, at heart, a eulogy. No one spends time at a funeral talking about how Aunt Shirley's kidneys failed and then blames her when the dialysis no longer worked. We might mention how a lifetime of smoking or the inhumane conditions of a coal mine led to Grandpa Joe's lung cancer, but we spend most of the funeral luncheon talking about his stubborn love and terrible jokes. A life is so much more than the facts of a body's failure.

At a funeral, we spend time naming how loved and loving our deceased ones were to us. We tell stories about their character, their complicated relationships, their contributions and significance, their quirks and curiosities. At funerals, we speak eulogies. The word "eulogy" has its origins in Greek, the roots of which are *eu*, meaning good, and *logos*, meaning words. A eulogy contains *good words* about someone who has died, words that serve as a tribute and praise, words of gratitude, and commendation.

In this book, I hope to speak *good words* about a community of people who knew what it meant to be the church. They understood that being a Christian congregation meant following Jesus, serving their neighbors, bearing one another's burdens, worshiping with authenticity, and being a people of deep welcome. As they aged and their congregation grew smaller, they realized they could no longer be the church as they understood a church was meant to be. They made the courageous, faithful, and utterly heartbreaking decision to give themselves away, to die so that new life could emerge for them and for countless others.

This book speaks good words, bearing witness to the faithfulness of the people of St. Peter's Lutheran Church at the end of their congregation's life. It's an extended love letter. I'll focus on the parts of our story that shaped this decision, as we named the hard realities, wrestled with the best way forward, and then stepped toward the end with hope. With the gift of time, I can tell the ways that our ending gave birth to all kinds of new beginnings, not just for the people of St. Peter's but for others all over this world. It's my prayer not just to bear witness to the faith of a little church in New Jersey but also to give hope to others who are, or who have been, a part of a congregation that has ended its ministry.

When I am preparing for a funeral, I spend considerable time with the family of the deceased. We discuss all the details of the day, which hymns we'll sing, what scripture will be read, and who will speak the eulogy. After we discuss all those logistics, I ask them to share stories. Tell me about your mother, I say. I knew her as the tiny powerhouse who unloaded cartons of wine as our one-woman altar guild, but what made her laugh? What stories do you tell over and over again about her character? What made her angry? What food do you eat that reminds you of her? How did she live her faith?

I ask to hear these stories not only to inform my funeral homily but because telling stories heals us. In telling our stories, we sort the chaotic mess of our grief into manageable piles of meaning. Both the painful and the hopeful moments become bound together in a deeper goodness. We discover patterns and connect the dots between experiences. In making space to acknowledge and feel emotions, storytelling moves us to the deeper layers of our experience where the treasures have been buried.

As people of faith, our storytelling has a particular throughline. We attach our stories to God's great big story of bringing life and healing to this world. It's a story first known in scripture, which we still discover and enjoy every day. God's great love for this earth and humankind began at creation, but the echoes of "This is good! This is very good!" continue to this day. Just as God brought liberation to the Israelites enslaved in Egypt, God still brings freedom from that which binds. The One who brought resurrection joy and amazement to some women at the tomb continues to bring hope to grieving and fearful people. God's ancient love story did not stop at the last sentence of the book of Revelation. It still echoes in the forgiveness given at bedsides, in the first steps a widow takes to claim a new life, and in a congregation's final acts of generosity as it dies.

In funeral homilies, our words become like stained glass windows. Vibrant, ancient biblical stories are soldered together with lived experiences, bringing God's acts of mercy into visibility. As the light of mercy shines through those stories, we see how God is still at work in the same ways we read about in Scripture, bringing people from death to life, from endings to beginnings, from fear to courage.

With a similar intention, a biblical story anchors each chapter of this book. Each of these stories functioned like a life preserver thrown to our congregation as uncertainty and grief tossed us around in deep and rough waters. The biblical stories originate from two sources: the stained-glass windows in St. Peter's sanctuary and the faithful hearts of the leaders of St. Peter's. Throughout our planning and discernment, members identified how specific passages of scripture offered them meaning and hope. In them, we found we were in good company, accompanied by God's people who have wandered in the wilderness, made tough decisions, endured hardship, and faced seemingly impossible futures. We remembered what God *has done* for and among God's people, and what God *will do, is doing*, even now.

This is a true story, but it is not a manual or a guidebook. It's my story of being a pastor to a people who courageously faced their greatest fear with courage and hope. No step-by-step map exists for closing a church, as every congregation facing the realities of closure knows. Each denomination has its own unique process. This book won't provide instructions, but it can expand imaginations. It will introduce companions on the journey who can say, "We've been there. The road is hard but not impossible. God is faithful and will bring you to new life on the other side. Just listen, we'll tell you."

This book is not prescriptive. It is not, in any way, a call to close more churches. Not every small church needs to end its ministry. Many tiny congregations are doing enormously important work in this world—mustard seed places of bold witness. We can be faithful with a little and faithful with much. As communities of faith, regardless of our size, we all ask the same question my Dad, also a pastor, would often ask: "Given this reality, how do we make the gospel known?" There are countless answers to this question, as we know from the many small congregations making Jesus known in beautiful ways.

But one of the given realities of these times is that churches are closing. This truth is heartbreakingly hard for those who lead and love these communities, and even more so for those who have invested their entire lives in them. However, stories of endings are not narratives of failure. They are testimonies of faithfulness. God remains active in these congregations and their people. God will continue to bring good news to them and through them. Stories of congregational closures are not just ones of despair and defeat but of generosity and courage.

I am not an expert on church closings, although some pastors and other faith leaders have received training and practice in accompanying congregations through the closing process. These leaders, like hospice nurses and hospital chaplains, lean into the brutal and beautiful realities of death and endings, doing so with intentional training and real grace.[1]

This story is uniquely mine. The details are as accurate as I can remember them. They grow from my perspective, with the clarity and cloudiness of time's passing. I only hope to be as faithful to the truth as I can be and not to harm the members of St. Peter's who entrusted themselves and their stories to me. I've recreated the dialogue as accurately as I can, based on my memory. In respect and care for the community I served, I've changed the names and some details of the people at St. Peter's, many of whom are now sainted, the flames of their candles dancing on All Saints' Day.

The words ahead are a eulogy, good words about a faithful people and an even more faithful God. When I light that candle for St. Peter's on

1. One of the best resources of support is the Good Friday Collaborative: https://www.goodfridaycollaborative.com/

All Saints' Day, I remember the courage and generosity of those people. I remember how the congregation trusted Jesus' promise that every ending leads to new beginnings. In dying, we live.

1

Summer 2006

David

But the Lord said to Samuel, "Do not look on his appearance or on the height of his stature, because I have rejected him, for the Lord does not see as mortals see; they look on the outward appearance, but the Lord looks on the heart" (1 Samuel 16:7).

The trees surprised me. I imagined New Jersey as a place of only traffic, highways, and endless concrete. But on my first visit to the state, driving a rental car out of Newark Airport, the bright green of woods along the interstate shoved those assumptions right out of my head. The trees of the Garden State, appropriately named, lined up like a welcoming committee. I was driving to an interview at a little church about an hour west of New York City. St. Peter's Lutheran Church, a small congregation in North Plainfield, needed a pastor. The leaders within our denomination, who serve as matchmakers between new pastors and congregations, thought I'd be a good fit. As I drove from the airport along the leaf-lined interstate, the unexpected shades of green became the first of many revelations that there was more to this state, this little town, and this congregation than I first thought.

Before that visit, I had a few phone conversations with Charlie, the council president and chair of the call committee. In his 50s, Charlie had recently been laid off from his job in the insurance industry. He used his unfortunately found extra time to usher his congregation into its next chapter. In our conversations, I could hear in his voice how much he loved the church and how proud he was of who they were in the world. They had weathered some conflict but cared well for each other. The congregation gave themselves away, sharing their money and their time for the sake of others. They could not afford a full-time pastor on their own but had received a redevelopment grant from our national church body to bring in someone who could help turn the decline around and move them into viability. Like Charlie, the leaders of our denomination saw the big-hearted faith of this small congregation. They saw in me the leadership qualities that fit their needs.

I took a break from my last weeks of seminary studies and flew east to New Jersey for an interview. After navigating the complicated streets outside the Budget car rental lot, I found my way to the tree-lined interstate. Despite being surrounded by eight lanes of cars and so many people, the hallway of trees created a sense of being in a forest. "I could live here," I thought, surprising myself.

After turning off the interstate to meander through the curvy roads of the Watchung Hills down to North Plainfield, I stopped at a light on Highway 22. Looking left and right, I saw the New Jersey I expected to see—so many people, cars, businesses, and endless cement. But as I crossed the highway, I entered a distinctive little town that would soon become home. North Plainfield covered less than three square miles of land, with a population of around 20,000 people and its own fire and police departments, library, and school district. Stony Brook, a meandering creek, wound its way through the town. The neighborhoods comprised a mix of large and small homes, with some boasting well-tended yards and others displaying peeling paint. Spanish and English signs adorned the restaurants and shops along the central business district that had clearly seen better days but was still bustling with activity and people.

The congregation I soon met bustled with activity and ministry, though it, too, had seen better days. Sunday School rooms, once full of children, now sat empty, with only a handful of little bodies of various ages combined in a single room. The choir sang each week, though fewer than a dozen people sang in four-part harmonies. A once-full sanctuary now held thirty people for worship on a good day. Like many other mainline

Protestant congregations in changing neighborhoods, St. Peter's membership had shrunk considerably.

On a tree-lined residential street just a few blocks from where the Stony Brook gently curved, I found the place that lured me across the country. Here was the little brick church with a sign on the front lawn saying, "The Welcome Place." Before I turned off the engine of my car, Charlie was right there to greet me. The message on that sign proved to be more than just a marketing campaign.

It wasn't just Charlie with the warm welcome. In that short visit, I had the opportunity to meet most of the congregation. They opened up easily, inviting me into their homes and freely sharing their stories and hopes. An eagerness and shyness blended, as if we were on a first date, each hoping the other would like us.

Turns out, the Spirit was already pulling us together. Just as those trees lining the interstate caught me off guard, this community surprised me with their vitality and goodness. They invited me back for another set of interviews, and during this second visit, my husband, Clark, accompanied me. After I preached that Sunday morning, we talked with members of the congregation over an impressive spread of desserts. When it came time for the vote to call me to be their next pastor, Charlie ushered us into the small, wood-paneled office. Assuming the vote would go in my favor, we remained at the church so we could celebrate together.

Clark sat in a metal folding chair. I took the more comfortable office chair. Simple gold-colored stained glass, cut in a diamond pattern, cast a warm glow into the room. The wood-paneled walls, it turns out, were not only dated in appearance; they were anything but soundproof. We could hear every word from the sound system that amplified the voices from the Fellowship Hall.

Perhaps it was my youthful pride and naivete, but I expected a quick and straightforward vote of approval. Instead, the deliberations took a considerable amount of time. I heard Charlie speaking in his clear, confident voice, discussing my qualifications. I had his trust and support, a reality that proved, for too short a time, to be a gift to me.

Following Charlie's presentation came a lengthy discussion. I didn't know the people enough to recognize their voices, but they spoke up and expressed their minds. I would come to learn that not only was this a New Jersey thing, but it was part of the culture of that congregation. They trusted each other enough to speak honestly with one another. But this bluntness was new to me. I'd been shaped by a Midwestern niceness that often kept the hard truths unsaid. Like new couples having to learn each other's ways of disagreeing, it took me a while to come to appreciate the forthrightness of many in the congregation.

But that day, I heard the muddled sounds of loud voices, which were hesitant, if not outright opposed, to my being called as their pastor. The resistance mainly seemed to be about money. Was it smart to spend what little resources they had left on a full-time pastor, and a young woman at that? Did I have what it takes? Would I be worth it? Could they afford even a basic salary?

Clark and I sat in silence as we listened, looking toward the voices as if we could see through the wall. I felt myself shrinking into the worn, checkered linoleum floor. Those questions hurt. I struggled to avoid taking them personally. Tinges of a kind of sexism that I and many other women, especially young women, face as leaders in the church were evident. And yet, the congregation had good reason for their reluctance. Money was in short supply. I had little professional experience. On the surface, calling me as their full-time pastor was not a good idea.

As I sat in the light of the sun coming through those diamond-shaped windows of the office, my mind wandered to the other stained-glass windows of the sanctuary. The people of St. Peter's had done an excellent job of introducing me to their building. They took pride in the space and its purpose. It was clear that this building shaped their community.

As I waited, spinning anxiously in that office chair, I thought of the stained-glass windows and the stories they illuminated. Most of them were installed in the 1950s and told the story of Jesus, from his birth to his ascension. A set of newer, more artistically unique windows was added in the 1970s and 1980s, using modern design, clean lines, and bright colors. Those new windows in the side transept of the sanctuary depicted three biblical men in profile—Peter, Elijah, and David.

In his window, David stands turned to the left, wearing bright blue and purple robes and strumming a small harp. His face in profile, David looks up with wonder and hope, like someone ready to burst into song. A sword sits positioned upright at his knee. Above him, the window declares, "I will sing to the Lord a new song." With harp and sword, this David is ready for both battle and praise.

As we know from the biblical story, the singer and shepherd named David wasn't the first or best choice to be the king. When God's people searched for their next leader, the Lord led Samuel, the priest, to Jesse's family to choose from among his sons. Jesse lined them up in a line, like the Von Trapp children in *The Sound of Music,* from oldest to youngest. He presented the obvious choices first—those strong, smart, and capable-looking older sons. Samuel looked at these impressive young men, convinced that God would choose from among them. But God surprised Samuel, whispering words that changed his criteria. Don't look at the outside, but pay attention to the internal substance. It's the heart that matters.

Jesse's handsome and hearty offspring passed in front of Samuel, but God spoke no words of affirmation for any of them. When pressed if he had any other sons, Jesse called his youngest boy from the fields. David had been tending to the sheep, overlooked and excluded from the lineup because of his age and small size. Despite his stature, the Spirit descended upon David that day and chose him to be the next king.

The Lord looks not on the outward appearance but on the heart. The Spirit has a unique set of requirements, none of which are based on age, gender, or physical strength. It's the heart.

Perhaps it was the Spirit's nudging that allowed the people of St. Peter's to look beyond my youth and inexperience to what was within. The vote to call me as their pastor passed decidedly, but not unanimously. In hindsight, I'm less hurt by the no votes and more amazed at the courage of that majority who voted yes. They had very few resources, yet they took a chance on me. Doubling down on an uncertain future, and with a risky hand, they went all in for me to be their pastor.

But my naive idealism took a hit that afternoon while sequestered in the church office. I had my first awareness that our ministry together would have its challenges. I would not just be walking through green pastures and peaceful waters. I'd need to be like that stained-glass David with not just a harp, but also a sword; ready not just for singing praise but for battle. There'd be no outright war, but we would face conflict and challenges. But I'd be in the company of people who knew how to sing praise to God and who saw and trusted the heart.

Later in David's story, his brothers left him behind to watch the sheep as they went off to fight in the war against the Philistines. Trusting that God, who rescued him from bears and lions, would be with him, young David volunteered to face off with the giant Goliath. As he prepared for that battle, David tried on King Saul's heavy armor and bronze helmet, only to take it off because it didn't fit or suit him. Unburdened, he stepped toward the giant wearing only his shepherd tunic, carrying five worn stones and his slingshot. Eugene Peterson writes that David "was both modest enough and bold enough to reject the suggestion that he do his work inauthentically (by using Saul's armor), and he was both modest enough and bold enough to use only that which he had been trained to use in his years as a shepherd (his sling and some stones). And he killed a giant."[1]

As I accepted this call to be their pastor, I prayed that I could be like David. I didn't have to be anyone but myself, with my own harp and sword. But I wasn't the only one underestimated and in need of confidence. The people of St. Peter's knew themselves to be small and not as well-resourced as other larger congregations. They, too, would need a dose of David's tenacity.

David took down a giant because he was both bold enough and modest enough. He didn't try to be anyone but himself. He trusted his experience and trusted the God who would empower him. The people of St. Peter's had many gifts and deep faithfulness. Yes, they were small and growing older, but they had a remarkable fierceness, generosity, and trust. It was loud enough, bold enough, that I had heard it right from the beginning through the thin walls of that wood-paneled office.

Small congregations possess such strength and beauty. They have ways of doing ministry, building relationships, and acting in faith that are not accessible to large churches. As I began my ministry, I trusted that we'd be able to do deeds just as unlikely as a young shepherd boy killing a giant with just a handful of stones.

Yes, we had huge battles ahead of us. It wouldn't be Goliath staring us down, but a deficit budget and a changing reality. We needed to find a way to make the congregation sustainable, reach out to our neighbors, and keep living out the love of Jesus. At the beginning, I was unaware of the depth of the challenges we'd face or the barriers we'd encounter. I didn't know enough even to be afraid. Full of youthful optimism, I didn't comprehend the size of the giant before us. But I also had no idea of the myriad, unexpected blessings God would bring to earn our praise. I did know, because it was loud enough to hear through the walls, that this was not a congregation to be underestimated. We were ready for both battle and praise.

1 Peterson, *Five Smooth Stones*, 21.

2

November 2006

The Shepherd and the Sheep

Jesus told them this parable: "Which one of you, having a hundred sheep and losing one of them, does not leave the ninety-nine in the wilderness and go after the one that is lost until he finds it? And when he has found it, he lays it on his shoulders and rejoices" (Luke 15:3–5).

On a November morning, as the clock counted down the minutes until the funeral service began, I stood panicked in the sacristy of St. Peter's. Athletes have locker rooms, but churches have sacristies where items for worship are kept and where leaders prepare. Ours should have had a funeral pall, somewhere in those wooden drawers, but I couldn't find it, anywhere. I had only been the pastor at St. Peter's for a few months. I'd only been a pastor *anywhere* for a few months. That morning, as the tables of the fellowship hall were being set up for the luncheon and the choir rehearsed, I dug through the drawers and the closet, holding back tears, desperately searching for that white pall.

But, in truth, the tears weren't really about the pall. Someone surely could locate the precious white blanket that drapes coffins. The pall would be found that morning, but I wasn't sure if there was a real pastor to be found. I looked at my reflection in the mirror, flanked by row of felt church banners. I saw a young woman wearing a designer black suit, thrifted from

Goodwill, topped off with a white clergy collar. She looked competent enough. But beneath the buttoned-up wool beat the racing heart of someone who had never officiated at a funeral, someone who would soon be expected to speak a word of life to a community she had quickly come to love.

I had experienced similar doubts of competence two weeks earlier, the last time I saw Charlie. Now I was about to officiate his funeral. Two weeks earlier, I stood in that same place, filling the vessels of my newly minted home communion kit with little bread wafers and sweet Mogen David wine the church had in the cupboard. I remember praying I could offer a measure of peace to Charlie and his wife, Katherine. Now I wondered if I had the right words for our community in grief.

I carried that little leather communion kit through the winding blocks and tree-lined streets of North Plainfield to a home that was familiar to me. As council president and the chair of my call committee, Charlie had been the first to invite us to dinner. In my early months at St. Peter's, I'd witnessed Charlie's steady, firm, and wise leadership. The congregation trusted him, and through his support of me, they looked to trust me as well. His support lent confidence to me when I doubted myself. Because faith anchored Charlie's life, it didn't surprise me when he requested that I pay a visit to their house to pray with them before his upcoming heart surgery.

I sat with Charlie and Katherine on their cozy floral couches in the house where they'd raised their family. They talked about their fears and anxieties, their much-adored grown sons, and their hopes for the little church where they'd invested so much of themselves. I read a few psalms, prayed, and then clumsily shared communion from my miniature travel set. Tears came easily to Katherine, though all our voices wavered as we prayed the Lord's Prayer together. Despite many uses of that communion kit now, it remains a beautiful mystery how the tiniest bit of wine and bread, paired with ancient words, can fill people with such outsized peace. I said goodbye and expected to see Charlie recovering in a hospital room the following day.

But that holy meal was my last one with Charlie. The following days were mostly a blur for me. I remember only that I received a call that there had been complications in surgery and that Charlie had died. Only that I wept and listened and sat with Katherine and her gentle, heartbroken sons. Only that I saw, not at all for the last time, the way the congregation knew how to care for one of their own. They showed up, arriving at Katherine's door with aluminum containers full of baked ziti and plates of brownies, tissues and prayers, presence and shared memories.

I had never presided at a funeral before. My internship, which was required in my denomination, took place at an international church in Moscow, Russia. While my time with the people there prepared me in many ways for pastoral ministry, I never had the opportunity to conduct a funeral. I needed help. So, I called my godfather Brian, a pastor in Seattle, for some advice and care.

Through tears, I told Brian about Charlie. I described his strong, easy leadership that anchored our church. I talked about the tall, white, athletic socks he wore with sandals, the sweatband around his head when doing work around the church, and the way he took time to know everyone. Brian listened as I shared how much Charlie meant to me and how I wanted to honor his life, offering comfort not just to Katherine and her sons but to a congregation who lost their good friend and leader.

Brian walked me through all the logistics, working with the funeral home, where the casket might be placed, and how the procession into the service would unfold. But then he said, "A funeral is about three things: remembering the person who has died, remembering and supporting one another, and remembering the promises of God. Your job is to shepherd your people through these three things. Simple."

Like many churches, St. Peter's had a stained-glass window depicting Jesus as the Good Shepherd. In one hand, Jesus holds a hooked shepherd's staff. In the other, Jesus tenderly carries a small lamb. You might not think that a stained-glass sheep could display trust in their face, but it was there, a look of reliance. The window depicts Jesus' parable about a shepherd who had one hundred sheep, only to discover that one of them had wandered away. With peculiar commitment to that one wayward sheep, he looks high and low for her. Carrying her back to her flock, the shepherd calls his friends together to celebrate the sheep's return.

The words of this parable and other lost-and-found parables shaped the lyrics of the hymn "Amazing Grace." Katherine chose the words of that hymn as the inscription for the inside of Charlie's casket. It became an obvious choice to sing at his funeral. "Amazing grace, how sweet the sound. I once was lost, but now I'm found." Our Good Shepherd finds us, carries us, and holds us in this world and the next.

Old hymns uniquely provide comfort. The familiar songs create a well-worn path from our sorrows to our joy, our despair to our hope. Like a shepherd carrying a sheep, singing those hymns brings us home. Our rituals and traditions remind us that we are not lost, but held by something strong, even as the world falls apart. I had come to know myself the confidence nurtured by these gifts of faith. The rituals and stories of the church carried me through the ups and downs of my growing up. I leaned into them my whole life, through weekly worship as a pastor's kid. They proved to be the bulwark I needed through life's struggles and the funerals of grandparents and friends.

But I experienced the real sturdiness of those rituals a few years before my time in New Jersey. The spring before I started seminary, my dad, a pastor himself, found out he had bone marrow cancer. The disease and its treatment wreaked havoc on his body, leading to his death just months following his diagnosis. Every night, throughout those weeks of chemotherapy, sickness, and hospice, my dad prayed what is known as Compline, or Night Prayer. He prayed the same prayers every evening at home or in the hospital, alone or with anyone by his side. The simple service begins:

> Almighty God grant us a quiet night and peace at the last.
> It is good to give thanks to the Lord,
> To sing praise to your name, O most High;
> To herald your love in the morning,
> Your truth at the close of the day.[1]

After reciting psalms and reading scripture, Compline ends with words attributed to Cardinal John Henry Newman: "O Lord, support us all the day long of this troubled life until the shadows lengthen and the evening comes, and the busy world is hushed, the fever of life is over, and our work is done. Then, in your mercy, grant us a safe lodging, and a holy rest, and peace at the last, through Jesus Christ our Lord. Amen."[2]

The words "peace at the last" bookend the Compline service and were our hope and promise in Dad's illness and dying. They held us, like the shepherd of Jesus' parable holds his lost sheep. When we couldn't make sense of our reality and when we felt lost to the power of death, disease, and isolation, the regular recitation of ancient prayers called us home. They carried us, not only back into the embrace of God, but into a flock of people who loved us. God will, indeed, bring us peace at the last.

1 Evangelical Lutheran Church in America, *Evangelical Lutheran Worship*, 320.

2 Evangelical Lutheran Church in America, *Evangelical Lutheran Worship*, 325.

After my dad died, the fever of his life turned to a cruel silence, our family sat around our dining room table to plan his funeral. The director for worship and music at my dad's church walked us through the planning. Tom described how the service would begin with cloaking the monastery-crafted oak casket with the white baptismal pall my mom had woven decades earlier. The beautiful white silk draped his casket with nothing less than the promise of God's love. That grace had been poured over Dad's head when he was baptized, carrying him into that safe lodging of God's eternal love. Then, as the congregation sang the first hymn, we were to follow the cross and casket into the sanctuary and take our place in the front pew.

"O God, Our Help in Ages Past" would begin the service. I wanted to ensure I had what I needed to sing this hymn as we processed. I asked Tom about making sure we'd have bulletins so that we could sing the harmonies. But Tom said, "Just let the community sing for you. At that moment, and maybe for a while, you might not be able to sing or pray, so let them sing for you and believe for you, even when you can't. Let them carry you."

Tom was right. The morning of Dad's funeral, as my family walked in procession, I was too choked up to sing. But the voices of the community around us held me, carried me. Friends, relatives, and parishioners continued to be present for us in the months to come, to be our voices when our own cracked with tears or grew silent in doubt. Surrounded by a flock, held in the care of our Good Shepherd, I was lost and found.

I certainly didn't grieve my dad's death alone. A broad community of people prayed for us, with us, and on our behalf. Years later, when I called Brian for guidance on my first funeral, he reminded me that I wouldn't have to bear the weight of Charlie's funeral on my own either. The people of St. Peter's weren't unfamiliar with funerals. They had already proven their ability to show up for Katherine and her family. This was a congregation that knew how to be the church for one another, to live in resurrection hope.

The little sheep in Jesus' parable didn't only have the joy of being held by her Good Shepherd. As the story has it, she was returned to her community. The promise of amazing grace doesn't consist of Jesus only, or even mostly, holding us individually close to him when we're broken-hearted or lost. We are held in community. We are found and restored to a flock.

As I stood in the sacristy the morning of Charlie's funeral, I remember Gloria coming around the corner, pantsuit precisely pressed, her hair curled into a perfect bob. She served on our worship and music committee, led the Altar Guild, and meticulously cared for all the precious items used for worship. With the well-polished communion chalice in her hand, Gloria turned and said, "Pastor, I took the funeral pall home last night. I wanted to make sure the creases were all steamed out. It's at the back of the sanctuary, ready for you."

I took a deep breath. The pall, once lost, was now found. I was not alone in this. The people of St. Peter's had spent decades accumulating knowledge of truths they'd need to remember. Over the coming years, through more funerals, and even our last goodbye, I would witness the community carrying one another, finding lost things, and trusting stories of new life.

3

DECEMBER 2006

The Nativity

And the Word became flesh and lived among us, and we have seen his glory, the glory as of a father's only son, full of grace and truth (John 1:14).

ON A WINTER'S EVENING soon after Charlie's funeral, my cell phone rang from a number I didn't recognize. I answered, only to hear the voice of Vinny, a member of St. Peter's. Vinny lived with his family a few blocks from church. His daughter, Maggie, took part in confirmation and served as an acolyte on Sunday Mornings. Despite his rough exterior, Vinny had a rare gentleness. He is one of the few Dads I've known who volunteer to lead their daughter's Girl Scout troop. That night on the phone, he told me in his thick New Jersey accent that there was a fire at the church. Without bothering to ask any questions, I hung up and was on my way, imagining the worst as I drove. But thankfully, as I crossed into North Plainfield, I saw no glow of flames from a ravaging fire. Multiple fire engines took up the streets around the building. Firefighters milled around outside, showing little urgency or worry. I breathed a huge sigh of relief. It couldn't be too bad.

As I walked toward the building, I spotted Roy heading in the same direction. Despite his age, 84-year-old Roy led the property committee, or, I should say, he *was* the property committee. Tall, broad-shouldered, but a bit stooped, Roy probably shouldn't have even looked at a ladder, much less climbed one. He'd been around St. Peter's since getting married in the now-familiar sanctuary well over fifty years ago. A retired locksmith and a skilled woodworker, the guy could fix anything. St. Peter's was his second home, a place he tended to like a spouse caring for the ills and aches of an aging partner.

Roy greeted me with a relieved smile. Vinny had called him, too. He heard the news of this fire, not only fearing the damage this fire could have caused, but also well aware of the last time St. Peter's had a fire. That 1946 fire, which destroyed most of the original wood-framed sanctuary, was due to faulty electrical wiring. Roy remembered bringing his wife Grace and her parents into the burnt remains of that old building and just crying. The pipe organ had been destroyed along with a beautiful, back-lit stained-glass picture of Christ that stood at the front of the sanctuary. The sacred space had provided refuge to the congregation through the Depression and two world wars, but the fire obliterated it on that day in 1946.

When the community came together to rebuild the sanctuary, they turned to brick construction. With the frugality of their time, the congregation recovered what they could from the original building. Grace remembered later, "Believe it or not, our present pews had been in the fire and were charred. But Mr. Krienke refinished them, along with our altar."

Sixty years later, Grace and Roy received another call about yet another fire. Vinny must have called him, too. As we walked together toward the fire chief, Roy moved slowly; his back hunched in a permanent curve. He seldom let on about the pain he felt in his back, where shrapnel still made a home, ever since a wounding at the Battle of the Bulge. When the fire chief saw us, he gave us a relieved smile. "The fire's out. Some repairs and a lot of clean-up ahead, but we got here quickly, thanks to them." He hooked his thumb toward Vinny, standing beside Maggie and a group of pre-teen girls on the sidewalk. I then remembered that their Girl Scout troop met weekly at our church on this particular night. Our building had been saved by the Girl Scouts! There must be a scout badge for responding fast to emergencies.

The next morning, Roy, Vinny, and I pulled out the damaged ceiling where wires from a light evidently caught the insulation on fire. We talked as we cleaned. I tried to convince Roy that, despite all evidence to the contrary, my Minnesota Twins were a far superior baseball team to his New York Yankees. He told stories. Roy tended to be quiet. Grace could talk enough for both of them most of the time. But that morning, as we scrubbed the black stains of smoke off cement block walls, he talked and talked about his work at the church. At first, he just replaced locks. In time, he joined a larger group of men who tinkered and worked around the building. After retiring, he took on larger projects, especially as the congregational workforce shrank. I'm sure he knew the intricacies of that building as well as he knew those of his own home.

When Roy talked about the building and its various additions over the decades, the conversation was laced with stories of his sons, their families, and, of course, Grace. He had the tenderest way of describing spaces where children learned the stories of Jesus, where music was created, where people served others, and where lifelong friendships were forged. He seemed eager to tell me exactly how volunteers managed to squeeze a shower stall into one of the bathrooms. I paid close attention, realizing this was some of what allowed the congregation to host a shelter ministry, an act of much labor and even more joy. Guests without homes who found their way to St. Peter's had all that they needed.

Buildings are the keepers of our stories. They're enormous photo albums and history books. The brick building on the corner of Mercer and Grove streets bore witness to countless weddings, baptisms, funerals, festive parties, dinner theater productions, and Sunday School programs. It was a literal home for dozens of unhoused people who found warmth and care when they needed a safe place. Inside those walls, lifetimes of moments were recognized, birth and death and everything in between.

Stepping inside the church door and inhaling the smell of wood polish, candles, and old carpet had a way of pulling people into the memories of all those moments. Touching the cement block walls with their layers of paint connected them with the generations who chose those paint colors. The sounds of shoes on linoleum and the echoes of the organ on the walls united the past and the present. Even a taste of coffee, somehow both watered down and too strong after sitting in a percolator for too long, pulls us back to a place, a space of sacred memory.

Churches embody our history, both the holy and the mundane. They are brick and cement books full of stories of God's people. The walls are their own dog-eared pages, highlighted with bulletin boards and sometimes cheap sacred art. Feeling the pew cushion connects us right back to the quiet kindness of the person who gave us candy to quiet a tickling throat or a restless preschooler. We unfold the creaking metal legs of folding tables and remember the gentle hands that pulled us out of the front of the potluck line with quiet instructions to hold back and wait until the guests, and then the older ones, got their food. The scent of dish soap and the force of water at the kitchen sink connect us to the old man, apron barely reaching around his ample belly, who told terrible jokes while washing dishes after spaghetti dinners, turning a chore into a joy. We learn the stories of faith not just from Sunday School and sermons, but from images in windows, symbols carved into wood, the embrace of familiar light, all in the spaces where we know we belong. A building is so much more than just a structure.

Whenever scripture describes a human encounter with God, we can pretty much bet that that place will be marked as holy. In those moments, people set down a kind of holy flag, like rocks with brass plaques along highways. After Hagar fled from the cruelty of Sarah, God met her in the wilderness and wrapped God's presence around her like a blanket. There, Hagar became the first human to name God. At that location, a spiritual and literal oasis between Kadesh and Bered, is a well called "Beer Lahai Roi," that is, "the well of the Living One who Sees Me" (Gen. 16:14). When Jacob wrestled with God, God knocked his hip out of socket and gave Jacob a new name. Jacob, now Israel, didn't just walk away from that place with a limp. With the stones he used for a pillow, he built a small altar and named that place "Peniel," which means "the Face of God" (Gen. 32:30).

Later, after lugging around the tablets of the law in the gold and winged tabernacle, the people of Israel longed to have a permanent place to keep that holiest of objects. They wanted a temple. In a move that could've been politically motivated or perhaps divinely inspired, David decided that instead of having little altars all over, people would come to one central place to meet God. At first, God didn't buy into this idea. With his dissolute living, David didn't do much to help his case, so it wasn't until Solomon's reign that God's people got their wish. In the temple, the people of Israel came to pray, offer sacrifices, and encounter the Living God. The psalms are full of stories of pilgrims, going to the temple in Jerusalem, "I was glad when they said to me, let us go to the house of the Lord" (Ps. 122:1).

Holy places matter because they hold our stories—our sacred stories. Our sanctuaries are where we meet God, where we experience grace, and where we come to know forgiveness. Inside their familiar walls, we make promises about our deepest commitments. Beginnings and endings happen there. We remember over and over again who and whose we are. Like

Hagar's well and the stones of Jacob's pillow, sanctuaries are places where God has comforted and confronted us.

Winston Churchill is famous for saying, "We shape our buildings, thereafter they shape us."[1] The spaces we build form us into the people we become. In a speech to the House of Lords, Churchill requested that the House of Commons, which was bombed out during the Second World War, be rebuilt. But not just rebuilt, rebuilt exactly as it was before. Churchill understood the profound impact of a building on shaping communities, forming identity, and instilling meaning. Buildings used for worship confirm this identity-making power as much as any other structure, in part because of the nature of their use. Architects intentionally plan light and angles, material and sound, to form a space of beauty, inspiration, and holiness. It's not just how it looks, but how it functions. Buildings inspire people to act and be what they hope to become.

The people of St. Peter's repeatedly sought to create spaces that would shape them into people of generosity, faith, and hospitality. After they rebuilt the sanctuary after the fire, the congregation added offices and classrooms. In 1960s and 1970s, when the Sunday School rooms filled to bursting, a large Fellowship Hall and more classrooms offered more places for learning and building community. The most recent addition came in the 1980s, when a large gathering space was built to connect the sanctuary to the Fellowship Hall, creating a place for hospitality before and after worship. Tacked on more for utility than architectural sophistication, these spaces were not particularly unique or beautiful, but they provided space to serve, to learn, to grow, to play, to connect. This is their beauty, how they came to matter so much. As the congregation planned and saved for these projects, their internal motivation was never just to erect a building, but rather to create special places of formation, spaces where people would be shaped.

Among those projects was the installation of stained-glass windows, telling the story of Jesus in images. In the Bethlehem window, a scattering of stars surrounds the Holy Family. Joseph's forehead wrinkles with worry. Mary holds the baby Jesus, her eyes staring off in the distance, perhaps pondering in her heart the words of the shepherds and angels. The infant Jesus of this window is depicted with chubby baby arms, belly button exposed, and curly hair. His feet evoke the miraculous wonder of an infant's tiny toes. His little hand holds up two fingers in blessing.

1. Churchill, *House of Commons Rebuilding*, para. 1.

The window depicts not just the birth of a baby but also the central truth for us Christians: God chose to get close and be born in human skin. The adorable toes in that window name that Jesus is God incarnate, Immanuel, God with us. God is no longer confined to heaven. God doesn't only meet people in designated holy places or altars of stone. Instead, God lives among us, a tabernacle of flesh and bone.

Following Christ's death, resurrection, and ascension, God sent the gift of the Holy Spirit, promising that God would abide with us forever. God's presence was no longer confined to one place but unleashed into the world, in and among God's people. As Paul wrote to the church in Corinth, "Do you not know that you are God's temple and that God's Spirit dwells in you?" (1 Cor. 3:16).

Faith doesn't demand that we erect church buildings. Christ is present where two or three of us assemble, anywhere. Since the beginning, people have worshipped wherever they could. Faith happens, mercy is shown, and grace is given on street corners and hospital rooms and around dining room tables. What matters are the people present, the body of Christ. In community is where Christ seems most pleased to dwell. Do you not know that you are God's church? We are the Lord's house.

Some of us sang in Sunday School: "The church is not a building; the church is not the steeple; the church is not a resting place; the church is the people!" And those words are true. "I am the church, you are the church, we are the church together, all who follow Jesus, all around the world. Yes! We're the church together."[2] This simple but memorable song names the reality of our ecclesiology. If we had no church buildings, we could still be the church—following Jesus, drawing together for worship, serving the world, sharing the Gospel. Countless congregations, without buildings, do brilliant and faithful ministry all over the world.

And, at the same time, our buildings matter. They make space for people to connect, where songs are sung, and meals are shared. Buildings shape us. They hold our stories, they carry memories, and house some of our most important moments. They help us see each other, God, and the world in the light of grace. For all these reasons and more, sacred spaces possess special value. They matter deeply to people.

That winter morning, the one after the Girl Scouts saved the day, I heard in Roy's stories what the deeper meaning of this little brick church offered its people. His boys had been so comfortable in that building that

2. Marsh and Avery, *I am the Church.*

one day, when Grace practiced with the choir, his youngest son had fallen asleep curled up in the hollow of the high pulpit. With a twinkle in his eyes, he said he couldn't tell me about the rest of the mischief those boys had gotten into over the years in the nooks and crannies of their second home. But Roy did quietly share that, after his return from Europe, he found healing by sitting in the familiar pews, week after week, surrounded by stained glass windows, beautiful music and people who cherished him. All the important events of his life had taken place in that space—weddings and baptisms, and too many funerals to count.

A few weeks after the fire, with the wiring and ceiling repaired, the community came together to decorate for Christmas. The blue Advent banners of glued-together felt came down to make room for Christmas trees on either side of the altar. With still a faint smell of smoke in the building, teams of people draped lights on the green boughs and hung pearl and gold-beaded Christmas ornaments on the trees. These Chrismons—sparkling crosses, alphas and omegas, trinitarian circles and doves—were made by families in the congregation many years before.

Worship on Christmas Eve contained the familiar slate of carols, along with the story of angel choirs and our Savior wrapped in swaddling cloths. When the time came for communion, our attention turned toward the altar, which had survived the fire and had been restored by Mr. Kreinke decades before. The congregation showing up that night had endured their own real and metaphorical fires throughout their lives. In gratitude and hope, I sang the Eucharistic prayer for Christmas:

> In the wonder and mystery of the Word made flesh
> you have opened the eyes of faith
> to a new and radiant vision of your glory,
> that, beholding the God made visible,
> we may be drawn to love the God whom we cannot see.[3]

In the newborn Jesus, the image of the invisible God is known. Still, now, whenever people assemble in a sanctuary around a table set with bread and wine, somehow Christ shows up, present in ways we can taste and see. But Christ is also made visible in the elderly locksmith, bent over, with metal in his back. He's there in the children thinking more of Santa than shepherds; in chintzy Christmas ornaments, in the wood pews refurbished, and in the art of stained-glass windows. The incarnation invites us to see

3. Evangelical Lutheran Church in America, *Leader's Ritual Edition*, 270.

God's presence in the material things of this world, bodies and creatures, trees and the soil—and buildings.

After communion, before we lit candles in the dark, Roy's wife, Grace, stood up, her white hair set in a halo of curls, and sang "Oh, Holy Night." She'd done this, from that same spot in St. Peter's sanctuary every Christmas Eve for decades, before and after both fires, her own life routinely restored just like those pews. The melody rose in Grace's confident soprano tone just as it had when she wasn't sure if her cherished soldier, Roy, would return from the front in Europe, later while her young sons slept in the pews (or pulpit), and after they left home on their own adventures. And she sang it again, her voice reverberating from the ceiling that had sheltered her for her entire life, the love of God echoing in our ears, adding another layer of hope and history onto the walls.

4

2007–2008

The Good Samaritan

[Jesus asked,] "Which of these three, do you think, was a neighbor to the man who fell into the hands of the robbers?" He said, "The one who showed him mercy." Jesus said to him, "Go and do likewise" (Luke 10:36–37).

THROUGHOUT MY YEARS AT St. Peter's, a group of women met for Bible Study every Wednesday. We sat in metal folding chairs as we talked about the passages of scripture that would shape our worship for the upcoming Sunday. Beyond learning about and from the Bible, the five or six women and I wrestled with matters of faith, navigated challenges in our lives, and discussed happenings in our community. Honest and often hard conversations shaped our time together; the women were not afraid to move into deeper waters.

One day, as we talked, I could tell Hilda had something on her mind. Despite being in her seventies, Hilda led our quilting group and coordinated our one-room Sunday School. She understood her role as a Sunday School teacher to be much more than just telling Bible Stories and doing fun crafts. More than once, a parent called on Hilda to pick up their kids after school or to drive them to piano lessons. She became an adopted grandmother to families far from their own biological families.

A tall and sturdy woman, Hilda wasn't afraid to speak her mind, often with humor and self-deprecation, her German accent always evident. She emigrated to the United States as a child, and much to the delight of all of us, didn't hesitate to swear in German if the situation demanded it. It was strange that day, when Hilda seemed to be holding back. I asked her what was on her mind. Hilda said, "I have been thinking a lot about dying." Then she paused, measuring her words. The rest of us waited to see what she was going to say. With timidness that was utterly out of character, she said, "I want to know what heaven is going to be like."

I thought for a minute and gave a response that I'm sure wasn't particularly helpful. It was likely more suited for a seminary paper than our little circle. But other women around our rectangular folding table weighed in about their own understandings of heaven. None of this seemed to comfort Hilda.

"Okay," she said, taking a deep breath, finding the courage to say what was actually bothering her. "All these hymns we sing, week after week, have words about how we will sing with the angels for eternity. I hate to sing. I mean, really, I loathe it. I can't imagine singing for the rest of time." With sincerity and a bit of fear, she asked, "Will I have to sing forever in heaven?"

I could see the relief it gave her to ask that question. An honoring quiet settled around us. Then, Grace, with her white, set curls and slim features, who already had a voice of an angel and would be content to sing every minute of eternity, said, "I'm sure you won't have to do something you hate in heaven." Then a teasing smile came over her face. "Or maybe, there will be some divine intervention, and you'll just love singing."

With a familiar guffaw, Hilda laughed. "I can get my head around the resurrection of the body, but not even Jesus could do the kind of miracle that could make me like singing."

We laughed together and talked about miracles, singing, and eternal life. The women shared their fears and hopes about what would happen when they died. I listened as they confidently shared God's power to hold them, especially through challenging times and rough circumstances.

I often felt a dissonance in being a pastor several decades younger than my parishioners. I was well-versed (pun intended) in the Bible, its languages, context, and history. I delighted in sharing that learning, shaping conversations, and being trusted to teach what God might be saying to us in those ancient words. But the wisdom and life experience of those women taught me new insights every time we studied together. They modeled for me what a life grounded in scripture looks like. And not just that, they showed me how to look squarely at the reality of death.

I remember when Grace went to the hospital for heart surgery. As with any cardiac procedure, Grace and her family worried. It was a precarious operation for an octogenarian, and after Charlie's death, even the most routine surgeries brought added fear for our people. I went to the hospital to pray with her before the surgery, and I arrived just as they were signing all the paperwork.

The surgeon walked her through all the risks and how tenuous her situation was. As he did so, Grace's anxiety seemed to increase by the second. She asked him, "Doctor, will I survive this?" The surgeon said, "I can't promise you that. You're getting older and surgery is complicated. But I promise I will be with you to the end. I do this every day. I'm the best one around." I almost laughed at his arrogance. But Grace immediately relaxed. It made no sense to me, but I was grateful for the peace in her eyes.

A few days later, I was sitting with Grace as she recovered. I asked her about the surgeon's arrogance and the subsequent peace she showed. Grace laughed, "He really was full of himself, wasn't he?"

She went further: "It wasn't his confidence that brought me peace. I heard him say, 'I'll be with you to the end.' And in that moment, I remembered Jesus saying those same words. And no matter what, whether I lived or died, Jesus would be with me. So, I wasn't afraid anymore. I knew I was in good hands." Then she laughed some more. "And I don't just mean that surgeon's hands."

In the United States, we routinely deny, ignore, and diminish the reality of death. So many of us refuse to talk about it. We convince ourselves that with enough technology, medicine, exercise, or moral living, we can somehow avoid death or at least postpone it until we're ready for it. Yet because of their own frail bodies or personal losses, the women in our Bible Study had already faced death head-on. They weren't afraid of it, and because of this, they weren't afraid to live.

We met together for Bible Study every week. Most of the women were retired, ranging in age from the youngest in her sixties to the oldest in her nineties. Our conversations began on the glorious days when I first started, and everything seemed possible. New ministry ideas began as scripture inspired us. In response to our varied griefs and worries, this circle of women helped instigate our first Blue Christmas service. People who were mourning or struggling during the holiday season received the gift of quiet and prayer, candle lighting, and healing hymns. Thanks to Katherine, who worked in the schools, members of St. Peter's soon began reading in our local school. We showed up every week to support teachers, read with kids, and provide another layer of care for our neighbors. One day, after our study, Clara and I knocked on doors around the block, getting to know our neighbors. After noticing a guest's confusion during worship, we reformatted the bulletins to make our liturgy more accessible to newcomers.

Our Bible study kick-started some new ministries, but it also created space for honest conversations about the challenges. The women shared their concerns about the amount of money being drawn from the endowment, the lack of participation in our ministries, and the fact that the same few people were handling everything. As they grew to trust me, I heard about the conflicts that simmered at St. Peter's over the years. A push and pull over leadership and decision-making led to lines being drawn. Divisions grew and personalities clashed. Distrust of pastors and institutions festered. Thankfully, the interim pastor who preceded me had worked to heal the division and tend to the wounds, but some hurt and wariness remained.

One afternoon after Bible Study, almost two years into my time at St. Peter's, a few women stopped in front of the bulletin board just outside the offices. The bulletin board featured the usual items—a community calendar, sign-ups for altar flowers, and flyers announcing upcoming events around town. The display included photos that celebrated various ministries over the years. Snapshots of refugees from Cambodia and Laos as they were welcomed were tacked to the corkboard, along with pictures of the Fellowship Hall set up with beds for families without homes. In the middle was a piece of fabric art from Chile with little dolls dressed in brightly woven clothing that surrounded colorful letters: EPES.

"Did you know that we were some of the first people to support the EPES community health programs in Chile, Pastor?" Grace asked. I did know, but I let her tell me, again, about how the congregation first met Karen Anderson, a Lutheran medical missionary from Minnesota. In the 1980s, she initiated EPES (Educación Popular en Salud, or Popular Education in Health), a program aiming to improve healthcare and living conditions for the poorest communities in Chile. With the help of congregations like St. Peter's, Karen set up a clinic, trained local women in basic health practices, and provided educational opportunities for children. Standing in the hallway that day, Grace proudly shared St. Peter's decades of support and partnership with this ministry in South America. Even when we had to draw money from our endowment to pay our monthly bills, the congregation never missed sending a check of support to provide for Karen's work among the Chilean people.

In the gathering space outside the sanctuary entrance, a stained-glass window depicts the story of the Good Samaritan. In classical style, a man leans back on a rock, nearly naked, his face gaunt from hunger and abandonment. Next to him stands the Samaritan, looking down compassionately at the man, a bowl of food in one hand, and perhaps a loaf of bread in the other. Behind him is a blue horse or donkey. I would sometimes amuse myself by calling it the Paul Bunyon Good Samaritan, with Babe the Blue Ox in the background.

The horse may not have been biologically accurate in color, but that didn't matter. The people of St. Peter's saw this story as central to their faith. When someone asked Jesus, "Who is my neighbor?" Jesus told this story about a man who was beaten, robbed, and left to die. A religious leader and an exceedingly pious man walk right by him, ignoring the man. But then a Samaritan stops to help. For Jesus and his friends, a Samaritan came from the wrong side of the tracks and the wrong religion. He would be the last person from whom they'd expect anything good. Yet, as this well-known story plays out, he tends to the beaten man's wounds, brings him to an inn, and steps up to pay for his care.

The question Jesus asked his interlocutor was legendary: "Which of these three, do you think, was a neighbor to the man who fell into the hands of the robbers?" When the questioner replied, "the one who was merciful." Jesus told him, "That's it. You got it. Now it's your turn. Go and do likewise" (Luke 10:36–37).

Long before I showed up on the scene, the people of St. Peter's had spent decades "doing likewise." Clearly, the message of that Paul Bunyan Good Samaritan became baked into their DNA. They lived with generosity and a commitment to show mercy to people who needed it. They were not perfect, but they understood that if they were going to follow Jesus, they had to give themselves away. For this particular community, a commitment to charitable love and generosity was as important to their lives of faith as convening for worship, singing, sharing coffee, and studying scripture.

A few years into my time at the church, I noticed a heaviness and sadness in certain conversations that members would initiate. They'd share the glories of their homeless sheltering ministry of the past, then shift to disappointment about how it had to end because of the decline of volunteers and the shortage of people to arrange and set up beds and cots. If it was the altar flower signup, they'd name the preponderance of empty slots waiting for people to donate Sunday bouquets. With pride, our people shared about the remarkable ministry with refugee families and teams of people who showed up to rebuild after disasters, but then sighed that they no longer could do any of it. Even the annual spaghetti dinner and variety show, which raised money for local non-profit organizations, had to be retired after key leaders moved.

"We're just a lot smaller than we used to be," Tillie said as she spoke for others in the church hallway that day. She shook her cane. "And older."

Grace, with a loving, faithful, honest heart, then spoke a word of truth. "We know what it means to be the church, Pastor Sara. Just look at this bulletin board. We know how to be generous and welcoming and serve our neighbors. We've done it. But we're getting older and there aren't many of us left. We know how to be the church. We just can't do it anymore."

5

2008

Young Jesus at the Temple

Jesus said to them, "Why were you searching for me? Did you not know that I must be in my Father's house?" But they did not understand what he said to them (Luke 2:49–51).

Two years into my time at St. Peter's, I sat at my desk, working away on my computer. The pastor's study, as it was called, sat near the side door of the church. The official front entrance was located on a busy thoroughfare through town. But most of our people parked on the side street and came in through the side entrance. These were dignified church doors, solid slats of wood painted red with the crown of a Gothic arch. On humid days, the wood expanded, making it stick in the frame. I'd regularly hip-check the door to close it, or tug on the elegant, iron door handles to make sure they latched. Those handles had small fish carved into them, a symbol from our namesake, Simon Peter the fisherman, the one called by Jesus to "fish for people."

That day, I heard someone at those doors, jiggling their keys. I had been around long enough to quickly identify who was coming through the doors. It's not that we had only entrusted a few people with keys—quite the opposite. I joked that there were as many people with keys to the building as people with offering envelopes. Everyone, it seemed, had a key to that red door. And by then, I knew our people and their patterns.

I could usually tell who would walk by my office door before I saw them. Sometimes they announced themselves as they came in the building, but I also came to know the rhythms of their walking, or the jangle of their keys. But that day, I didn't know who was entering the building. The footsteps fell in an unfamiliar pattern. I rolled back my chair and turned to look through the doorway into the hall. There stood Hilda, all six feet of her, with a cane in one hand and a big garbage bag stuffed with finished quilts in the other.

Hilda was an indefatigable force, the engine behind our Sunday School, the quilters, and more. In her late seventies, she was the tall, German Energizer Bunny of our church, prone to profanity. She could not be stopped or slowed down. Hilda saw my eyes move toward the cane in her hand. Before I spoke a word, she lifted the cane and said something in German I couldn't understand. (Even if I had understood it, the words likely wouldn't be appropriate for print.) She looked down, unable to look me in the eye, and mumbled, "Better this than ending up in a hospital, I guess. The boys are making me use it. But I don't like it." (The "boys" were none other than her grown sons, showing thoughtful attention to their aging parent.)

I offered to carry the quilts to the shelves in the quilting room, piling them up with the rest of the quilts, sewn, tied, and ready to be given away. "I might need a cane, Pastor, but I can still get stuff done." (Though, of course, she didn't actually say "stuff.") Without apology for her expletive, Hilda gave me a resigned smile and slowly made her way down the darkened hallway—a new pace to her step.

Even Hilda was slowing down. Sure, she could still get "stuff" done, but not like she once did. While a quilt delivery and a new cane might not seem a dramatic turning point in most narrative arcs, that day stood out as significant. Things were changing and had been changing around St. Peter's. Hilda, with a cane, embodied that shift.

Despite the congregation's efforts over the previous two years, we hadn't experienced the growth necessary for sustainability. Reading in our local school, knocking on doors, inviting friends to church, attempting to build relationships with our neighbors, beginning various projects and programs under the leadership of our synod—none of this proved to be enough. Fewer people showed up for worship. Service opportunities stalled without the necessary leaders. We lacked the outcomes we needed. The grant money we had received from our churchwide organization to balance the budget and to help pay my full-time salary was running out. We had only so much time to change the direction of our decline before the money was gone.

By the summer of 2008, our congregation was limping along like Hilda. Along with other leaders, I'd been paying attention to the signs of our viability. Mostly, we tracked numbers. How big was our deficit this month? How much of our grant money is left? How many more months can we continue at this rate?

At our council's monthly meetings, we celebrated the congregation's continued generosity and regular worship attendance. Checks to EPES in Chile and our larger church body were sent off. Our support staff received the smallest of raises to honor their work. However, we began to regularly draw from our endowment fund to cover our bare-bones budget. A weight of worry would enter the room every time we even glanced at the trajectory of our financial resources. Mostly, though, leaders weren't willing to talk about the growing crisis yet. At least not publicly.

As I sat in the office, poring over numbers and brainstorming options for our congregation's future, I would often hear someone unlock the big red doors. The door to my office was always open. The small study was cozy, with stained-glass windows of yellow and green letting in a glow of light. Bookshelves lined one of the walls. The remaining space had just enough room for a standard metal desk, office chair, file cabinets, and a rocking chair.

I'm not sure who thought their pastor needed a rocking chair, but it provided delightful solace. Perhaps it's the peaceful movement of the gentle repetitive motion or the memories of being cradled as a child. In any case, many people found their way to that rocking chair in those summer months.

I couldn't begin to answer all the questions that came at me from that rocker. The big decisions were never mine alone to make. I didn't have a clear vision of how our future would unfold. Still, members of the congregation came, sat, and moved back and forth in that chair, processing aloud what they were noticing, experiencing, and worrying about. They shared their frustrations with our failed attempts to bring new people into the fold. They lamented the departure of former members of the congregation and tried to make sense of old conflicts. We brainstormed new ideas and confessed how stuck we were in limited ways of thinking or acting.

Sometimes people arrived for conversation too fired up to even sit down. With anger and irritation, they paced around my little office or stood glaring down at me as I sat at my desk. I listened to their complaints about something I'd done or not done. At other times, long-past transgressions by someone or some group needed to be rehashed. They found me, the pastor, to be the safe place to exhume all that anger.

Many of those conversations named a truth that I needed to hear, a truth that helped me be a better pastor. They provided feedback that led me to make amends and move us in a better direction. But other times, I was simply a repository, the anger so much more about the complainer than about me. At my best, I remained in the moment, imagining a polyethylene tarp over my heart to keep it from absorbing the anxiety and anger. I listened, asking questions to help move through the anger into a place of clarity or understanding. I'd pose simple questions or encourage more conversation. "What else?" "Tell me more." However, the downpour of blame and distrust often seeped through that tarp, sowing the seeds of personal doubt and shame.

We were all in a strange place. I'd been at St. Peter's about two years, long enough to know them well, but also still so new. Something was wrong, but nobody was sure what to do about the growing challenges, how bad they really were, or what would become of us. We knew we couldn't keep on going like we were, but we didn't know what needed to change or exactly when it would be necessary to take drastic action.

It reminded me of my own grandmother, Bette, who, upon discovering a lump in her breast, took several months before telling anyone about it, before seeing a doctor, before doing anything. She feared what she'd learn and worried about the news she'd receive. The uncertainty paralyzed her. This inaction frustrated our family. But in retrospect, I think Grandma Bette just needed some time to get her head around the realities she was facing.

For my grandma and the people of St. Peter's, uncertainty brought fear and worry. We could only see so far in front of us. The people of St. Peter's didn't rush forward, but we slowed down, almost to a stop. Like Grandma, we needed to get our heads around what was happening. And so they came into my office to rock, to talk, to share their worries.

George walked in often, and whenever I heard his heavy steps, I'd brace myself. Short and slightly balding, George always wore a perfectly pressed shirt and polished shoes, carrying a leather folder full of papers. He'd been at St. Peter's his whole life. A retired lawyer, George would question me in a way that felt like I was on a witness stand, being cross-examined about decisions I made or words I said. Usually, though, George would start with a question about budgets or meeting minutes as an excuse to engage in conversation. He talked about his law career and told me his favorite stories and quotes from Horace Rumpole, the fictional English barrister in books by John Mortimer. When George didn't support my ideas, he quoted old Rumpole, who said, "If I do not like the way the times are moving, I shall refuse to accompany them."[1]

As people rocked and remembered, they also shared what worried them most about the uncertain viability of their church. What would happen when they died if their church no longer existed? What happens to our quilters? How about our kids? Will I ever be asked to serve in leadership again? Is there a choir with whom I can sing? Bigger questions emerged, too, the ones whispered in the quiet of the night, but often hard to say in the light of day. Did we fail? Is God judging us? Do we matter anymore? Does Jesus have a stake in any of this? Will my investment live on? What is my legacy?

I had no answers, just plenty of my own questions. I struggled in these months as a pastor, lacking clarity about where and how to lead. My husband teased me that I was like the character Pigpen from the Peanuts cartoon, except that instead of a large cloud of dust, I walked around in a big cloud of confusion.

Around me, different voices offered contradictory guidance about the most faithful way forward. I met with our Bishop and his staff, who shared that the congregation and the neighborhood we served were too important to lose. They told me we needed to keep at it, that we couldn't give up yet. Admittedly, some congregation members felt this same way, though even they were growing weary of doing so much to keep us going. Others were disillusioned, or perhaps simply realists, believing that drastic action or decisive change was the only way forward.

In addition to seeking the wisdom and advice of plenty of thoughtful people around me, I read every book I could find on congregational change, revitalization, and renewal. Like a child hiding inappropriate magazines from his parents, I also privately read the few books written about closing congregations. Even contemplating this possibility felt like betrayal. Still, I combed through them, filled them with notes, underlined entire paragraphs, and put colorful stick tabs on important pages. But no map exists for how to lead a church through questions of its mortality. No one has created an easy step-by-step program for responding to rapidly declining congregational capacity.

1. Mortimer, *The Anti-Social Behaviour of Horace Rumpole*, 85.

I wished for a GPS to tell me exactly where to go and how to get there. I wanted someone to say: "Okay, Pastor, here's what you and your people need to do," like a basketball coach with a whiteboard outlining plays. Our synodical staff tried to be helpful, but they left this to be our journey. The congregation would make its own choices. Like my grandma had to initiate the all-important call to the doctor, they had to be the ones to name aloud reality and face it.

One of the old stained-glass windows at St. Peter's depicts young Jesus in the temple. Standing before a green curtain, the youthful Jesus has a smooth face, with no hint of a beard. Jesus leans on a wooden pulpit with a cathedral arch resembling St. Peter's own pulpit. Looking out to the viewer, his hand about to point, young Jesus seems about ready to speak.

Luke writes of Jesus and his family making a pilgrimage to the temple every year. When Jesus was twelve, he didn't go home with them. When his parents realized their son was missing, they rushed back to Jerusalem, terrified for their lost son. They found Jesus nowhere else but in the temple, deep in conversation with the elders. Others listened in, watching this boy with amazement at how much he understood. When Mary and Joseph see him among the wise leaders, both angry and astonished, Jesus says, "I was never lost, I was here, in my Father's house." Jesus was right where he needed to be, right where he belonged.

With the blessing of hindsight, I can now look back on that season at St. Peter's and see that, despite our lack of clarity or direction, we weren't entirely lost. We just didn't know exactly where we were going. Like young Jesus, we simply needed to keep spending time with God and God's people, listening and asking questions. But we did require some of Jesus' confidence to trust that we weren't actually lost.

Congregations in the midst of discernment often feel as if they're steering a car down a foggy road. They can't see much beyond the hood ornament, focusing on what's immediately ahead or keeping an eye out for a familiar landmark. With a limited view, this is what I could see: we were a small church, doing our best, without many resources. We were still making Jesus known. Still worshipping, still singing, and drinking coffee. Still making quilts and serving, canes and all. Still being God's people. Maybe we weren't lost. Maybe we just didn't know where we were going . . . yet.

After my father's diagnosis with bone marrow cancer, he had several rounds of intensive chemotherapy before he got horribly sick. It quickly became clear that all optimistic plans for effective chemotherapy followed by a bone marrow transplant would not happen. My parents scrapped the original treatment plan and worked with the doctors to find another route.

My dad, always with a book in hand, had been reading the journalist William Least-Heat Moon's book *River Horse*. Moon wrote of his four-month adventure riding America's rivers on a 22-foot boat. He narrated his encounters with the water, creatures, and people he met. In the cabin of his ship, Moon placed a sign with the words of a Quaker saying, "Proceed as the way opens."[2]

This became my dad's mantra during those months before his death. "Proceed as the way opens." He would make decisions as they became necessary, based on the realities that became known. Resisting the temptation to look far ahead, he faced every juncture with faithful, realistic hope. He tried not to force his way upstream or against the current. For my Dad, with his most uncertain and unknown future, this image of a river with a swift current carrying him along helped him relax into the moment. It gave him a way to trust God's presence to guide him, day by day, while life and death unfolded.

In those days of confusion and unknowns at St. Peter's, following the wisdom of William Least-Heat Moon and memories of my father's trust, I aimed to "proceed as the way opened." I didn't have to have all the answers. But we weren't lost. We were where we needed to be. Where Jesus sat in that temple, the people of St. Peter's sat in a rocking chair, listening, remembering, praying. As we rocked, we waited to see where God would lead us next.

2 Heat-Moon, *River Horse*, xvi.

6

2008

Palm Parade

When he had come near Bethphage and Bethany, at the place called the Mount of Olives, he sent two of the disciples, saying, "Go into the village ahead of you, and as you enter it you will find tied there a colt that has never been ridden. Untie it and bring it here. If anyone asks you, 'Why are you untying it?' just say this, 'The Lord needs it'" (Luke 19:29–31).

As the people of St. Peter's continued to proceed as the way opened, it became increasingly clear that our hopes as a congregation would not be realized. Worry over money and the ramifications of it running out creeped in. Anxiety grew and manifested itself in some funny ways, as anxiety tends to do. We had skirmishes over the frequency of communion and the possibility of renting out the building to others. People bickered about this and that topic, even as others deepened their empathy and listening with renewed care. Our people were tired, despite their steady commitment to doing the work of the church. I was impressed by their faithful attention to our common life together, even though I could see in their eyes and hear in their voices both present weariness and future worry.

The uncertainty took a toll on me, too. I started to seriously doubt that I had what it took. My confidence began to unravel, and my own anxiety increased. I loved my people and wondered if I was disappointing them, and not just them, but our synodical leaders and all those who had believed in me. Plus, I'd taken a few hits, in words, of course, from some of our leaders whose anxiety and grief showed up in anger and sometimes cruel words that diminished me. I began to wonder, in the presence of people I trusted the most, whether God had truly called me to ministry.

I recall my dad sharing a story that occurred when some of his pastor friends met together early in their ministry. They were each asked to share the best and the worst part of their work that month. Around the circle they went, talking about the good and the bad. Someone described a brilliant sermon they preached, but also a failed confirmation lesson they led. Someone else had a project that excited people but an excruciating confrontation from a parishioner. Each of them shared one recently great thing about their life as a pastor and one recently challenging thing. As they went around the circle, one of my dad's friends looked at his colleagues and simply said, "The people. And the people."

It's true for any of us, any time we find ourselves in an intentional community. The people. They're both the best and the worst, the easiest and the toughest parts. To share life with others is to be open to disagreement and conflict. Despite our occasional wish otherwise, the gift of Christian community is the people, the very same ones who can also make it challenging. When we are honest, though, each of us is part of that mix. Erasmus may have said it best, "Therefore I will put up with this church until I see a better one, and it will have to put up with me until I become better."[1]

Throughout my time in New Jersey, I met with a group of local Lutheran pastors to share my own struggles and joy. Our primary goal was to discuss scriptural passages related to our preaching for the upcoming Sunday. However, this preparation would usually deviate into discussing the happenings at our congregations, along with various worries and hopes. Not surprisingly, we shared the best and the worst.

One week, after hearing me describe the weight of uncertainty at St. Peter's, my colleague Fred said, "Sara, whenever I feel overwhelmed, I like to go and make some visits. Nothing will help you fall back in love with being a pastor more than forgetting about all the administrative tasks of the church and remembering the people."

Fred was in his 70s at the time. He almost always wore his white clergy collar and a threadbare suit coat that was just a bit too big for his thin frame.

1 Erasmus, *Collected Works*, 117.

With a stash of shortbread cookies in his car in case someone forgot to bring snacks, Fred also had plenty of wisdom and smart jokes to share. Raised in the more conservative Lutheran Church-Missouri Synod, he knew his Bible and had been active in the civil rights movement in St. Louis before making his way to the East Coast. He shepherded urban congregations and engaged in thoughtful, out-of-the-box ministry before ending his long career by serving part-time at a church a few towns away from me.

Fred spoke the truth and didn't mince words. He had a love for people and Jesus that I deeply admired. And so, in those months when nothing felt quite right, I took Fred's advice. I laid aside my spiraling discouragement and self-doubt and spent as much time as I could visiting the people of St. Peter's in their homes. This was no hardship or chore. For me, these visits to our older members always proved enlivening and grounding. However, during that particular season of my ministry, the visits served as a life preserver, allowing me to float when the waters became too deep.

Robert and Millie became one of my favorite pairs to visit. Millie could still make it to church, her purse full of candies to share with kids. They never had children of their own, but this didn't stop them from loving other people's offspring. By the time I got to St. Peter's, Robert's declining health had pretty much confined him to home. I know he would've loved to step into church again, if even to glimpse the stained glass. Their small house was on Gold Street, and they joked that they didn't need to die and go to heaven to live on streets of gold; they had it right in New Jersey.

Robert collected matchboxes and had hundreds of them. While he loved his collection, his love for those cardboard covers had much more to do with the people and places this hobby brought into their lives. Before I pulled out my communion kit and Bible, they would always bring out the match covers, those little colorful boxes became doors to stories about their shared adventures.

When Robert died, we held his funeral at the church he loved. Robert would be buried at a cemetery a few towns away from North Plainfield. After the service, we made our way to our cars for the procession to the cemetery. After taking off my robe and grabbing my prayer book, I got into my car, pulling in right behind the hearse, ready to make the slow, intentional journey to the cemetery.

As we drove, I thought about Robert and the people of St. Peter's. Robert died during that time of foggy uncertainty. My mind circled with worry. I was weighed down by all the happenings and unknowns at church—by the people and the people. I spiraled around situations where I wish I had acted differently, or where I felt hurt by a conversation. I thought of these people I had come to love, and felt weak and incompetent, unable to change the situation that led to our precarious reality. I had a lot on my mind, none of which is an excuse for what happened that day.

I almost ran out of gas during a funeral procession.

I hadn't even noticed my tank was close to empty, but as we drove south out of North Plainfield, I saw my fuel gauge on the dashboard sitting on the red line, then moving just below it. My little sedan didn't have the fancy technology that displays exactly how many miles a car can go before running out of gas, but I knew I was getting dangerously close. As our procession of cars drove past a gas station, I flipped off my emergency flashers and turned on my blinker. Rolling down my window, I waved the procession to go on without me, and, surely on fumes, pulled into the gas station.

The laws of New Jersey at the time provided me with grace that day. It's illegal to pump gas yourself, so I could sink low into my seat and wait for the attendant to fill my tank. I prayed no one in the procession would see me. After my car was refueled and I generously tipped the angel in greasy coveralls, I chased down the funeral procession, hoping I wouldn't be late for a burial service I was to lead.

Thankfully, the hearse had kept a slow and solemn pace. I pulled in as the caboose of the funeral procession well before we made it to the cemetery. Millie either didn't notice or was gracious enough not to mention it, but the funeral director smiled and kindly shook his head at my embarrassing misstep.

At our text study with colleagues the following week, I shared my gas tank story, partly to dilute my shame. We laughed about it, but I could see concern in a few of their eyes. The joking that ensued was healing, and a deep breath of reflection on my part allowed me to admit how tired and overwhelmed I felt. Feelings of failure poured out. It wasn't just my car running out of gas. I was, too.

Fred broke the quiet among that circle of colleagues by saying, "Sara. It's not all on you. It's never all about you." That was Fred, regularly reminding us of this truth, putting us lovingly in our place. Every time one of us pastors would say, "*my* church" (as in "*my* church started a food pantry" or "*my* church is running out of money"), Fred would interrupt: "It is not *your* church. It is *Christ's* church. You're just the pastor who serves there. Try again." And like dutiful children, we'd say, "The church *I serve* just finished its 100th quilt this year." "The church *I serve* might need to close."

Fred asked me if I was finding sabbath. "You are no good if you are running on empty. Take a break."

"But they need me," I said, stubborn in my commitment to my people.

Fred smiled and looked me right in the eye. "When I was younger, I was asked to interview for another congregation on the other side of the country. I loved where I was serving and didn't want to move. I told the district president I couldn't move and that the congregation I currently served needed me as their pastor. The district president responded, 'Fred, the only thing our Lord ever needed was an ass.'"

We laughed about this obvious reference to the donkey in the Palm Sunday story. Jesus asked his disciples to furnish him with a donkey for his final, triumphal entry into Jerusalem. Jesus knows that they'll surely be asked why they're taking someone else's donkey. His instruction (surprisingly satisfactory to the owner of that beast of burden) was to say, "The Lord needs it." It was true, the only time Jesus ever stated a need for anything, or anyone, it was for a donkey, an ass.

Fred was telling me to get over myself and not be an ass.

This message is on display at St. Peter's, where, in one of the sanctuary windows, Jesus is depicted riding a donkey. Whether his appearance is one of serenity or humility (or both), a radiant halo encircles Jesus's head. A few adults are pictured behind Jesus, mouths open in awe, or perhaps singing "Hosanna" with palm branches held high in their hands. In the foreground, children wearing bright clothes hold each other's hands and seem to be dancing. They, too, hold palm branches. The whole image is one of joy and awe, praise and thanksgiving. And in the middle of it all is a donkey carrying the Savior of the world.

I thought about that donkey and Fred's words a lot in the days that followed. The humor of his one-liner made me smile, but his words were convicting. I couldn't single-handedly save the church. I wasn't the savior of my own life, much less my congregation (the congregation I served). Believing I could fix it all wasn't only unproductive, it brought exhaustion and shame, turning me into something of a stubborn ass.

Jesus invited many people into adventures and a new way of life, but all he personally needed was a donkey. But how might I become more like that donkey? I figured I could stop trying to carry all those people, the best and the worst of them. I'd try to cease believing it was my job to fix, control, and protect them. Instead, I would focus on what I could do. I'd bring Christ's message of love and courage. Instead of meeting everyone else's expectations and responding to everyone else's needs, I would keep my actions simple. I'd be like that donkey, bearing Christ in my words, actions, and our shared work.

Mary Oliver wrote a lovely poem about that Palm Sunday donkey. The donkey compares himself to strong horses and beautiful doves. But comes to realize the gift of being just who he had always been—a small, responsive beast of burden. This was just what Jesus needed. The poem ends with the donkey's pondering:

> Still, he was what he had always been: small, dark, obedient.
>
> I hope, finally, he felt brave.
> I hope, finally, he loved the man who rode so lightly upon him,
> as he lifted one dusty hoof and stepped, as he had to, forward.[2]

Bravery and obedience. I wanted to feel a little more brave and trust that I was all I needed to be. I wanted to love and trust the One I was carrying (who carried me). So I stepped, as I had to, forward.

2. Oliver, "Poet Thinks about the Donkey," 44.

7

Summer 2008

Isaiah

Then I heard the voice of the Lord saying, "Whom shall I send, and who will go for us?" And I said, "Here am I; send me!" (Isaiah 6:8).

For nearly three decades, when anyone phoned St. Peter's Lutheran Church, they would hear the warm, Jersey-accented voice of a woman named Pam. She was the part-time church secretary, answering the phone and generously greeting everyone who walked through our doors. Pam had the unique combination of skills needed for her job. Gracious and hospitable, she was capable of all things administrative. Having been around for so long, she knew everyone and everyone's stories. She asked for updates on our members' grandkids and how the medicine was working.

Pam remained with the congregation through many changes, including the appointment of new pastors, the introduction of new hymnals, and the adoption of new technologies. While she used the computer for most of her work, the typewriter was her first, true office machine love. Occasionally, from my office across from hers, I would hear the click, click, click, click, whrrrr of the typewriter.

But, from my perspective, the real treasure of that office was Pam's box of clip art. Tucked into the shelves sat a short cardboard box, separated into small, labeled sections and filled with paper pieces of clip art that she had saved from decades of creating newsletters and bulletins. When working on the newsletter, she'd find perfect little black-and-white drawings with Bible verses or cute people holding signs like "Church Picnic Ahead!" or "A Blessed Easter to you!" or "Big News!"

I cherished my mornings with Pam during those days when our future seemed uncertain. When much of ministry felt like driving through an unknown city, doing familiar tasks brought solace. Even as we faced big questions about our existence, we still needed to answer the phones and mail out the monthly newsletter. The weekly bulletin had to be put together. Thankfully, these projects continued to happen with reassuring regularity.

While Pam and I found comfort in the routine of office work, the congregation found similar assurance while using those bulletins in worship. Week by week, Sunday by Sunday, the people of St. Peter's made their way to the church and sat in their same spots on those dark wood pews. Like Pam and her typewriter, the people of St. Peter's had proven themselves open to some changes in our life together, but they were pretty set in where they sat on a Sunday morning.

Periodically, many of our people would give up their usual seats in the pews to help lead worship. Twelve-year-old Ethan and his mom, Debbie, were a regular part of this rotation. We had only a small handful of youth to serve as acolytes, lighting candles and helping with communion. Ethan was a dependable regular in the rotation. Despite living almost an hour away, Ethan and Debbie rarely missed worship. When Ethan began middle school, Debbie quickly volunteered him to be an acolyte. He was the third generation of his family to serve in this way at St. Peter's. His mother and her parents were all raised in the church, and her grandparents were pillars of the place. The people of St. Peter's adored Ethan as they'd watched him grow up, making space for him to serve and thrive in his particular giftedness as a neurodiverse kid.

On the days he served as an acolyte, we searched for a robe that would be long enough to outfit Ethan and his fast-growing legs. I asked him about school, what he was reading, and about the music he was making with his musician dad. Right at 9:30, Debbie gave Ethan the nod, and he walked to a small vestibule on the side of the sanctuary. There, he untied the rope connected to the big church bell hanging high above him and pulled, ringing the bell with joyful, appropriate abandon.

For centuries, church bells have summoned people to prayer. Before cell phones, watches, or even clocks had been invented, communities relied on church bells to signal when it was time for worship. The first clocks were built not to inform banks and businesses when to open or when people needed to get to work; they were made so that people would know when to stop work and start praying. Church bells rang more as an invitation than an alarm clock. Like the strong voices echoing from the minarets of mosques throughout the Islamic world, church bells are a call to prayer.

In a Danish Lutheran church outside Luck, Wisconsin, the church bell has these words inscribed on it:

> Til Badet og Bordet,
> (To Font and Table)
> Til Bønnen og Ordet,
> (To Prayer and Word)
> Jeg Kalder Hver Søgende Sjæl.
> (I Call Every Seeking Soul)[1]

Our bell at St. Peter's had no fancy inscription. But whether Ethan or another adolescent stood ready to pull the rope, our neighborhood was about to be summoned to community, scripture, and song.

The Lutheran tradition is a liturgical one. It provides a familiar rhythm to worship that encourages participation, even as it transforms us into new ways of being. While the prayers or scripture change each week, other components of the liturgy stay the same. A pattern and flow remain. The prayers, repeated or spoken in unison, become a part of us. Written on our hearts, these words get memorized and embodied. Some days they might feel rote or repetitious, but it's like telling someone you love them, over and over again. We need to hear those words of affection more than once.

Worship is akin to dinners at our house with my children. We sit down together every night, though I sometimes wish for super glue to keep my fidgety kids in their seats. Silliness may land spaghetti on the floor, or the conversation may devolve into the latest fart joke, or we endure through dessert. But sometimes, conversation turns deep. Or adventurous. Or serious. The kids share, and we end up connecting in beautiful ways. These miraculous moments only occur because we sit down deliberately together every night, ready for the magical to spring from the routine.

Sometimes worship feels monotonous or as if we're going through the motions. Other times, we hear just what we need to hear. We discover ourselves lighter and more free, connected to others as we sing. A word of direction or purpose we've been praying to find mysteriously arrives.

1 Lathrop, *Holy Things*, 89.

Words are written in our hearts so that we can find them when we need them most. We could never get to those deeper places if we didn't intentionally stay through the times that felt mundane.

In those anxious days, when I felt the pressure of budget challenges and my inability to fix it all, I was particularly grateful for our liturgical tradition. I didn't have a lot of clarity about what to say to my people, so I leaned into the patterns, the words, the prayers of the church. People of faith had been praying them for centuries. They've proved their power. These practices have sustained people during chaos far messier than what we were experiencing. We were not the only ones unsure where we were going or how best to be faithful. The familiarity of these rhythms and words comforted us because they've weathered the storms. They have proven to be durable, steady guides through tragedies, heartbreak, and trauma. As my dad advised his colleagues and himself, "Just pray the ancient prayers, and let them do their work."

Singing was at the heart of our togetherness. Never mind that the instrument encouraging us was an aging electric organ (its sibling is on display at the Smithsonian). Julie, the organist, knew just how to coax beautiful music out of the beast and get us on our feet. Often in four-part harmonies, the people of St. Peter's sang with full voice and hope. Even in our discord, singing allowed us to breathe together. It's through song that we experience in our muscles, our bones, that we are not alone. We belong to a community bigger than our individual selves.

People of faith have been singing since the beginning. From Miriam leading the women in singing after finding freedom from slavery to David and his harp. The book of Isaiah is sometimes known as the "Singing Book," although it is also referred to as the "Suffering Book." The prophet Isaiah likely understood that singing and suffering were two sides of the same coin when it came to loving God and this world.

Among the collection of newer windows at St. Peter's was a picture of Isaiah. Like David, Isaiah is depicted in profile, with an angular face, severe cheekbones, and a long beard. He wears these yellow shoes, which look like fashionable loafers. Isaiah looks up with expectation and hope. His left arm reaches around his torso, toward us, and he holds one finger up, like he's telling us, "Wait a minute, something important is happening, I'll be right with you." He's preparing to be set on fire, literally and figuratively, by God. Having seen the magnificence of God sitting on the throne, while angelic beings sang "Holy, Holy, Holy!" Isaiah couldn't help but realize his own smallness and faults. But God doesn't cast Isaiah aside or chastise him; God directs the seraphim to retrieve a lump of coal with some tongs to touch, purify, and forgive Isaiah. And then God asks, "Who will go for us?" With lips burning, Isaiah speaks, "Here I am, send me."

Isaiah said yes to speak both judgment and hope to God's people. Pointing out hypocrisy and telling hard truths became his repeated call. But he also imagined a future of wholeness and possibility through God's regenerative grace. This is how Isaiah became known as the prophet of both singing and suffering. Envisioning a future full of restoration and healing, Isaiah spoke of a tree that had been torn down, burned, and abandoned, yet not dead. From that stump would come a branch, and from that branch a whole new, beautiful future, embodied in a Messiah who would bring abundant life to this world.

Week by week, Sunday by Sunday, like Isaiah, we stood in the hem of God's glory, and remembered those promises of God's sustaining presence. At communion, we repeated the chorus of those angelic beings so long ago, "holy, holy, holy!" Then we'd sing, "Christ has died. Christ has risen. Christ will come again." And with those words, we trusted that our lives are drawn into that paschal mystery—in dying, we live. In endings, somehow, we find beginnings. Our lives of faith are about practicing the truths that we will one day need. Like people preparing for disasters with cans of food and bottles of water in the basement, in worship we tuck inside our hearts the promises and truths of God that we might not need now, but we will someday need as provisions to nourish and strengthen us.

That summer, two years after I began at St. Peter's, we didn't make any big decisions, but we did worship. The sanctuary didn't have air conditioning, but still, we showed up, a sweaty, faithful bunch to sing. We prayed those ancient prayers and let them work on us. We stored those messages of promise in our spiritual storehouses, because we would soon need them.

Meanwhile, our financial resources shrank, and our worries grew. People sat in my rocking chair and shared their fears. And all the while, Sunday by Sunday, Pam selected the perfect clip art for newsletters and made copies of bulletins.

Until the copy machine stopped working.

It was the copy machine that got us talking.

Copy machines are essential to the work of most congregations. They place prayers, hymns, announcements, and scripture on paper every week. Those bulletins make for access and shared participation in worship. But it wasn't just bulletins that were made on that machine. We needed it for Bible Studies and Sunday school materials, council notes, budgets, and newsletters. We needed a copy machine to do the work of being the church. But one summer day in 2008, it just stopped working. It could not be repaired.

Our financial struggles had become apparent, but none of us felt ready to name the hard truth. But that changed when the copy machine broke. The company that serviced our old machine offered us a relatively good deal: a lease on a used machine and a service agreement with a multi-year contract. As our council discussed this copy machine lease, someone said, with cautiousness from both fear and sadness, "But will we be around for the whole length of this contract?"

This question prompted leaders to analyze the number of copies we made and compare options with other copier companies and big box electronics stores. At the time, I couldn't see the point of investing so much energy into discussing a copy machine. But the discussion wasn't about office equipment. The copy machine turned out to be the key that opened the door of the locked room we were afraid to enter. It provided a space to begin exploring what was surely to come. Facing that small decision led us to address bigger ones. Bearing a resemblance to Isaiah with that piece of coal on his lips, our congregation leaders began to speak aloud what had been in their hearts for months. "What is our future? What is realistic for us to plan for? What is our actual financial situation? How sustainable is all of this?"

We examined the data in front of us, not just the number of copies rolling out of the copy machine, but also the pledges received and the offerings shared. We analyzed how much we were drawing from our endowment each month and how long those withdrawals would last. Beyond the numbers, we discussed how people were doing and how weariness, aging, and capacity were affecting our ministry.

By the end of that summer, we had made two big decisions. The first was a technical fix. Thanks to a generous gift from a friend of the congregation, we purchased a modest copy machine that would meet our small congregation's needs. The second was an adaptive response. We formed a team of people whose sole responsibility was to plot the congregation's future. They would prayerfully examine all the options and then, given the realities that would emerge, lead the congregation in identifying the most faithful way forward.

And so it was, one Thursday morning, that Pam stood at our new little copy machine ever so slowly printing out Sunday's bulletins. Under a clip art saying "Big News!" we announced the first meeting of St. Peter's "Future Task Force."

8

Fall 2008

Abraham and Sarah

The Lord said to Abram, "Go from your country and your kindred and your father's house to the land that I will show you. I will make of you a great nation, and I will bless you and make your name great, so that you will be a blessing" (Genesis 12:1–2).

As a child, whenever I lost a tooth, I put it under my pillow and fell asleep with hopeful anticipation that the tooth fairy would come. While my friends discovered quarters under their pillows, I found an envelope with a story tucked inside. I ignored the evidence that the tooth fairy had handwriting remarkably like my father's angular slant, with the thick ink from the pens that left big black dots on the front pocket of his shirts. I read those stories, written just for me, over and over again.

The "tooth fairy" left me stories about a queen. But this was not a queen who worried about gowns or balls. My queen had grand and sometimes hilarious adventures. Looking back, I see that they were not just stories to entertain me but were written to shape me into a person of courage, kindness, and faith. I must have doubted myself because one of the stories described the queen learning to trust in her own unique gifts. Another story involved the queen discovering that her beauty was not in her looks, but in her songs. In another, the queen learned that her tears were a source of power, not a sign of weakness. The tooth fairy (spoiler: my dad) shaped me into a better person, not with lectures or instructions, but with stories about a queen who blew open my imagination of who I could be in the world.

As I grew up, I listened to my dad repeat this same way of formation from the pulpit of the congregations he served as a pastor. He shaped communities with stories. Sometimes he told about real people living bold lives of faith. At other times, his tales resembled my tooth fairy stories—fictional narratives that drew his congregation into a faithful imagination. He trusted that stories had the power to expand thinking and provide an experience of grace. Well-told narratives open the curtains of limited thinking enough to allow us to see ourselves and the world from new angles, enabling us to dream of a new kind of future.

Those stories didn't just come from his imagination. They grew out of the scripture that my dad learned by heart. Every Monday, my dad would sit with the designated gospel reading for the upcoming Sunday and memorize it. Dad committed to this for two reasons. Most importantly, it allowed him to proclaim the gospel reading at worship as it had been first intended, as oral storytelling. However, the secondary benefit was that the piece of scripture lived in my dad throughout his week. It'd be in his head and heart as he made visits, sat in meetings, answered phone calls, and ultimately, wove all those experiences together for his sermon. Dad shaped his whole week around a trust that stories change us, especially the sacred stories of scripture. Even when he took a leave from active ministry because of his cancer, Dad still memorized the gospel and other readings for the upcoming Sunday. He would not be preaching, but I think he needed those words in his heart to give meaning and grounding to his living, and then to his dying.

At least a decade before his death, Dad wrote a book about congregational leadership titled *The Evangelical Pastor.* He wrote about the power and importance of story in a pastor's life.

> [A pastor] allows the biblical story of God's faithful activity in and through the people of God to be a gift, a demand, and an invitation. The biblical story is a gift in that it announces that God graces all of creation with a promised identity that transcends even the brokenness of the world. The gift of identity is the source of all hope and meaning—the source of abundant life. Living in, under, and through the biblical story captures the pastor in the wonder of God's precious gift of life revealed in Jesus Christ . . . The spiritual

> life begins with living in and through the biblical story and hearing the invitation to conversion. To live in the biblical story is not only to receive the gift of identity, life, and love, it is to be transformed into a new person.[1]

As I prepared for our first meeting of the Future Task Force, I looked through all kinds of books on pastoral leadership and consulted so many resources. None of them had a lot of clarity about helping a congregation discern what to do when they were running out of time. I felt a bit stuck, and I did what I often did in those moments: I wondered what my dad would have done.

Stories. My dad would tell stories. He'd find ways to connect the biblical story to our questions, our hopes, and our worries.

Eugene Peterson wrote that a pastor's primary job is to be a story-maker, helping to provide meaning, scaffolding, context, and identity to our seemingly disjointed lives. "The pastor knows that the story of God's revelation is a comprehensive narrative that includes everyone . . . [biblical stories] provide the insights and incentive to get such persons to understand their own stories as chapters, or at least paragraphs, in the epic narration of God's saving history."[2]

While the Bible ends with the last verses of the book of Revelation, we trust that through the Spirit, God is still at work in the lives of God's people. We are the continuation of that epic story of God's blessing and saving this whole world. God is still doing what God has always done. Those stories of God's work before us can help us make sense of our own stories. Joseph Sittler wrote, "All things are bearable if we make a story of them. And ultimate desolations are made both more bearable and significant when the story is the Ultimate Story."[3]

As we faced the desolations of the possible ending of St. Peter's, I wanted to be intentional about weaving our stories into that Ultimate Story. The hard road ahead would only be bearable if we rooted ourselves in something, some One, so much bigger than ourselves. And so, at the first meeting of our Future Task Force, we began our time by putting ourselves into the biblical story—or rather, we put the biblical narrative into us.

That first meeting took place in the dining room at Katherine's house. As we sat around the table, surrounded by pictures on the walls and his

1. Olson, *The Evangelical Pastor*, 32.
2. Peterson, *Five Smooth Stones*, 76.
3. Sittler, *Ecology of Faith*, 39.

vast collection of glass bottles, we felt the blessing and memory of Charlie. Katherine, now the council president, thought it would be good to start our time together in a more comfortable space than the metal folding chairs and meeting rooms of the church. So, Katherine welcomed us into her dining room, held in the goodness of her graciousness and floral wallpaper. The team consisted of individuals specially invited by the church council, chosen for their expertise and experience. Others volunteered to join, forming a team with a good mix of ages, perspectives, and lengths of time as church members.

We prayed together after Katherine served tea and put sweet snacks next to the Bibles on the table. I began our work by asking the members of the Future Task Force to think about a part of scripture that connected with our situation. What biblical story is St. Peter's living right now? What story or idea from scripture describes us or our situation? Who in scripture faced similar challenges? Where did people experience problems or joys like ours? As they pondered their responses, some people flipped through the Bible, but most just sat quietly, prayerfully, thinking. After about five minutes of quiet and reflection, I invited people to share.

Around the table they went, telling stories, reciting verses they knew by heart, or reading from the Bible. They referenced scripture that resonated with them and that they believed mirrored our experience. As the Task Force continued to meet, we used the scripture passages shared that first night as devotions for our monthly meetings. Grounded in those chosen stories, we discussed insights we gained about God and ourselves, as we saw ourselves reflected in centuries-old narratives. At each of those monthly meetings, I would ask, "What do you think God was up to in those stories? What did the people do? How is God up to those same ways of mending and freeing now? What, then, might God be inviting us to do?"

As we went around the table at that first meeting, Hilda shared how she thought we were a bit like Abraham and Sarah. It was back when their names were still Abram and Sarai, before the time in Egypt, before the laughter, and before the birth of baby Isaac. Hilda might not have wanted to sing with the angels, but she certainly knew the Bible. She remembered God instructing Abram and Sarai to pack up all that they had and follow where God would lead them. They didn't know where they were going. They simply trusted.

The twelfth chapter of Genesis marks a pivotal point in the biblical narrative. The Bible begins with a grand panoramic view at the outset. But after the cosmic stories about creation, the fall of humanity, an epic flood, and God's covenantal promises, Genesis zeroes in on one couple, Abram and Sarai. When we read "now God said to Abram," it's suddenly clear that God's no longer just a cosmic voice echoing across the universe, but a conversation partner. God doesn't just speak the sun into being ("Let there be light!"), God speaks personally and intimately to a middle-aged couple. At this point in the story, all we know about Abram and Sarai is their genealogy and their childlessness. They haven't done exceptional acts of faith to capture the attention of the Most High God. Yet God wants to partner with them. Later, we learn of Abram's moral shortcomings, yet still, God focused attention and blessed both him and Sarai, and through them blessed the whole world.

What struck Hilda were those words God spoke to Abram (and Sarai), "Leave the place and people you know, and go to the place that I will lead you." God asked Abram and Sarai to walk away from all that was familiar to go somewhere not yet shown to them. Step away from the comfortable to an unknown place that God will eventually reveal. And, forward in faith, they walked, heading toward a place still not defined or known. Think of yourself speaking to a global positioning system: "Give me directions to some place I don't yet know." That was Abram and Sarai's predicament, and invitation.

They didn't know *where* they were going, but they did know *who* would show them the way. This was enough. After that conversation with God, Abram and Sarai never turned back. They began a journey not knowing where it would end, but only that God would guide them.

Hilda offered us a grounding story, connecting these biblical ancestors' confidence in their own unknown future with our present challenge. So many of the faithful ones who had gone before us had little idea where they were going. All they could do was step forward in faith. The evening of our first Future Task Force meeting was filled with stories that reminded us of the original promise in the Book of Genesis. The God who made the cosmos cared about us, even us. God would lead us through present unknowns to a place we had not yet discovered.

As for the agenda of that first Future Task Force meeting, we didn't just tell stories. We set some intentions for how we'd communicate, share honestly, and listen thoughtfully in this time of high anxiety. Our job was to develop recommendations for the congregation to consider regarding our future and sustainability. One of my dad's favorite questions, when he trained pastors and congregations, was: "Given this reality, how do we make the gospel known?" It ought to be self-evident to people of faith that we commit ourselves to sharing the love of Jesus and making the good news of his life known. But congregations answer this question in many ways. Every community, time, situation, and every combination of gifts and challenges will yield a different way of making the gospel known. To discern who we are called to be, we must first identify the situation in which we find ourselves. Then, since that reality cannot be easily altered, we can explore how to utilize our unique limitations and possibilities to make the good news of Jesus known.

Our Task Force addressed the first part of that equation head-on: What is our current reality? Leaders combed through spreadsheets to look at the deficits in previous years alongside current assets. We reviewed the membership rolls and giving patterns. Despite faithful generosity, giving had declined. Trend patterns matched the progression of aging within the membership, along with portions of the congregation moving away. The conclusion was stark. Barring a serendipitous miracle, we had about 18 months until the congregation would completely deplete its endowment and could no longer support the ministry financially.

But budget numbers were only one piece of the equation. We also discussed the capacity of our people to perform the necessary work to be the church, as well as the congregation's willingness to undertake projects or make changes that would make us viable. These questions could not be measured with a spreadsheet. But the writing was on the wall. All of us in leadership had noticed the weariness of our people and the workload carried by fewer and fewer people. It was becoming evident that we no longer had the capacity to do the work of being the church.

I remembered that conversation I had with Grace in the hallway so many months before, when she shared her outlook. "We know what it means to be the church, Pastor Sara. We just can't do it anymore."

Something needed to change. We couldn't keep going without making some big decisions. But what would those be? Around the dining room table at Katherine's house, we brainstormed the options: merge with another church, share a pastor, move our pastor to part-time, raise money from grants to cover costs, have another church merge with us, rent out our building, sell the building but rent a new space to stay together, or sell the property and disband.

As we discussed these options, people shared both positives and negatives. We tried to narrow down which options the team would explore in more depth. At one point, when one of the options looked to do little more than perpetuate our own existence, keep our resources just for us, and care only for our own people, someone around the table said, "But how do we keep going as a CHURCH?" I don't remember who said this, but I wrote it in my notes, in big letters, with CHURCH in all caps, underlined. They asked the question that deserved to be at the heart of our discernment: Isn't our existence about more than just continuing? How will our decision help us be the CHURCH? We can't just take care of ourselves, we're meant to do more.

The issue was coming into sharper focus: Given this reality, how can we be the church? We were getting clear on the stark reality, but it was still unclear how we would make the gospel of Jesus known. We desired to do more than just exist. What was emerging as consensus was that we were to follow in Abram and Sarai's footsteps, stepping forward to the place where God would lead us.

9

January 2009

Thy Will Be Done

When he reached the place, Jesus said to them, "Pray that you may not come into the time of trial." Then he withdrew from them about a stone's throw, knelt down, and prayed, "Father, if you are willing, remove this cup from me, yet not my will but yours be done" (Luke 22:40–42).

Over the coming months, the Future Task Force continued to meet. Colleagues at the Office of the Bishop were supportive but clear: the decision was ours to make. We had limited time, and the sooner we acted, the more options we had, the more generous we could be. Every possibility and eventuality was discussed. One night, we played the "yes, but . . . " game for every option. Yes, that's a great idea, but what about this? Yes, we could merge, but with whom, when, and how do we go about that? Yes, we could seek more rental income, but who would the tenant be, how much would we need, and how would we manage all of that easily? Yes, we could reduce our staff, but what would Sundays look like? For each one of those options, we also asked, "How does this one help us be the church? How does this help make Jesus known?"

By the time of our Annual Meeting in January, three possibilities emerged as finalists for consideration. 1. Merge with another church, Lutheran or non-Lutheran. 2. Reduce salaries for all staff, share a pastor with another congregation, or call a part-time pastor. 3. Develop a plan for a turnaround. It remains a wonder to me that the people of St. Peter's didn't add a fourth option: to hold on tight to whatever resources they had until the money completely ran out. They didn't even consider this. Nobody was willing to offer up the option to stubbornly stay for the sake of staying. Everybody seemed to cling to a deep understanding of what it meant to be a church, even though this commitment came at a significant personal cost to all of us.

The leaders of the Task Force presented those three options to the forty-some people present at our Annual Meeting. Then people came up to the microphone to share which one they thought would be our faithful way forward. Some members of the congregation expressed passionate hope yet deep grief. Others shared wild dreams, grasping at what I thought were impossible straws. Still others stewed in anger and disappointment. A few sat in quiet, exhausted resignation. While we reached no unanimity, community consensus seemed to indicate that merging or associating with another church would be the best option.

At the end of our meeting, as a few of us stacked folded chairs along the concrete block wall of the Fellowship Hall, I noticed that George didn't have his usual frenetic bluster. I asked him if he was okay. He thought a minute and said, "None of us wants this. But we've been praying since the beginning: 'not my will, but thine.'" The loquacious George couldn't usually be limited to just a sentence or two, but that's all he had to say. He turned and walked to help the others clean up.

At our first Future Task Force meeting, George referenced this same line from scripture. Those words were first spoken by Jesus, the night before he died, praying in the Garden of Gethsemane for the strength to do God's will. A window depicting this moment hangs in the St. Peter's sanctuary. In that stained-glass version of the famous Johann Heinrich Hofmann painting, "Christ in Gethsemane," Jesus kneels with his arms extended on the rock in front of him, his long fingers gently folded in prayer. In green and red robes, the bearded Jesus looks up toward the top left of the window, as a stream of light shines onto his face.

When George talked about Jesus' faithful prayer, I wondered how many times in life he must've peered up at that Gethsemane window. Seventy years times fifty-two Sundays a year, minus a few years in college and living in New York City, plus all the times beyond Sundays he showed up to work at church. I estimated that he would have looked at that window at least 3,500 times in his lifetime, likely more. Not our will, but thine. That window, this prayer, gave him, and all of us, courage to step forward.

Soon after that Annual Meeting, during Lent of 2009, we chose to orient the penitential season around the Lord's Prayer. I organized our adult learning to unpack each line of that familiar prayer and preached a sermon series on it. Using the assigned readings from the Revised Common Lectionary, I focused on a different petition each Sunday. In part, it was a crutch; it helped with my preaching preparation when our discernment process overwhelmed me. But I also wanted to let those ancient words work on us, to guide us.

When we pray "Thy will be done," we often see it as a consent to doing a specific, predetermined action God wants from or for us. It's as if God has a path for us, like breadcrumbs through the forest or a particular route on a GPS. "If it's God's will, I'll do it," we say, usually begrudgingly. Or we blame whatever tragedy or suffering has befallen us as "God's will." But the Greek word, *thelēma,* which is translated *will,* could also be translated desire, wish, or even dream. We pray that God's desires be done for us and all the earth, as it is in heaven. We pray that God's wishes come true, for each of us and the world.

This prayer is more than just a birthday candle kind of wish. "Will" has a sense of purpose. There's a driving intention behind it, a stubborn commitment. In our prayers, we name the powerful and transformative truth that not only does God desire good for this world, but God works for those desires to become known. With strength and perhaps a divine kind of pigheadedness, God is persistent in God's ways. In our prayers, we align our hopes with God's big hopes. We say we want God's dreams to be realized, even when seemingly impossible. We entrust our lives to God's unrelenting work to bring those hopes to fruition. In those months, we were all learning to let go of our own ways.

After the annual meeting, Katherine and I collaborated on a letter to be sent to the members of St. Peter's. We wanted to ensure that everyone understood the reality of our situation and outlined the next steps, including the possible merger or closure of St. Peter's. We wrote, "For the sake of Christ's mission in and beyond St. Peter's, many also wish to provide for the care of our building and possibly make other legacy gifts, should the congregation close. For this reason, many think it unwise to use the entirety of our funds." As the letter concluded, we wrote, "In all of this, the Future Task Force does not make decisions; it simply prayerfully considers and makes suggestions. The congregation of St. Peter's Lutheran Church—you—will make the decision that determines our future."

We had hoped that God would take the cup away from us, but we followed as we were led. "Thy will be done," we continued to pray. We hoped that somehow, in these decisions, just as St. Peter's had been for generations, we would help bring God's dream of goodness and life into this world.

10

February 2009

Noah's Ark

Then the Lord said to Noah, "Go into the ark, you and all your household, for I have seen that you alone are righteous before me in this generation. Take with you seven pairs of all clean animals, the male and its mate; and a pair of the animals that are not clean, the male and its mate; and seven pairs of the birds of the air also, male and female, to keep their kind alive on the face of all the earth" (Genesis 7:1–4).

The annual meeting gave us new clarity. We'd explore the idea of partnering with another congregation to merge or share ministry in some way, or we'd move toward closing. Two of the Bishop's assistants had accompanied us through my time at St. Peter's and the last months of our discernment. They offered resources and encouraged us. We needed their help in this next step, as we collaborated with neighboring congregations to explore what kind of shared ministry might be feasible.

A few Lutheran congregations were located nearby, and we thought they might be potential partners. This would take exploration. I had connections with leaders and pastors at these churches, including my husband, Clark, who served as the pastor at St. Stephen's Lutheran Church, a few miles away in South Plainfield. With the guidance from leaders in the office of the Bishop, Clark and I planned a "Regional Mission Gathering" for a

Saturday in February. Pastor Wagner, one of the assistants to the Bishop who had been a support for me since I started at St. Peter's, wrote in an invitation to our neighboring congregations: "Despite much good work, including significant growth in stewardship, the people of St. Peter's have serious questions about the ongoing viability of their ministry as it is presently configured. This prompted us to look at the situations of the nearest neighbors and consider the possibility of some conversations among the congregations about the shape and style of mission-oriented ministry that could include some cooperative and mutually supportive elements." The invited congregations were geographically close, but the budgets, values, and membership differed greatly. We hoped that by meeting together intentionally, we might find some common ground.

Many months earlier, when asked about Bible stories that resonated with our experience, Grace surprised me. With characteristic wisdom and simplicity, Grace said, "It feels like we are on Noah's ark, floating on the water, unsure of when or where we will ever find solid ground. We're sending birds out now, looking to see if there will be people to receive us. But we are safe, together, in the meantime." Then Grace looked at me and asked, "Don't they call a church sanctuary a 'nave,' Pastor, because it's like a boat? The church is like Noah's ark, a safe shelter for all of us, right?"

I nodded. For centuries, architects and theologians have likened the church to the ark, a holy vessel that carries God's people to salvation. Scandinavian churches often have intricate model ships hanging from the rafters. Frederick Buechner's description of this church as the ark is memorable:

> In one as in the other, [churches and the ark] just about everything imaginable is aboard, the clean and the unclean both. They are all piled in together helter-skelter, the predators and the prey, the wild and the tame, the sleek and beautiful ones and the ones that are ugly as sin. There are sly young foxes and impossible old cows. There are the catty and the piggish and the peacock-proud. There are hawks and there are doves. Some are wise as owls, some silly as geese; some meek as lambs and others fire-breathing dragons . . . It's not all enjoyable. There's backbiting just like everywhere else. There's a pecking order. There's jostling at the trough . . .
>
> But even at its worst, there's at least one thing that makes it bearable within, and that is the storm without—the wild winds and terrible waves and in all the watery waste, no help in sight. And at its best, there is, if never clear sailing, shelter from the blast, a sense of somehow heading in the right direction in spite of

> everything, a ship to keep afloat, and, like a beacon in the dark, the hope of finding safe harbor at last.[1]

St Peter's was, in so many ways, that kind of place, full of both the best and the worst. Amid the heightened anxieties, we had fire-breathing dragons and silly geese, wise owls and meek lambs. We were a menagerie of people. Yet, we rode the waves and the storm together, sheltered from the flood. As I anticipated our meeting with these neighboring congregations, it seemed to me we were sending out ravens and doves, trying to see if there would be a safe place to land.

Our first raven sent out was the invitation to this Regional Mission Gathering. We hoped this raven would come back with some sign that there was a place, a people with whom we could partner. Three of the four invited congregations showed up, along with two assistants to the Bishop. The raven had performed the first part of its flight assignment. It took off.

The day began with worship that included the prayer, "Direct us, O Lord, in all our doings with your most gracious favor, that in all our works begun, continued, and ended in you, we may glorify your most holy name, through Jesus Christ, our Lord. Amen."[2]

That prayer sentence echoed in my head throughout the day and in the days that followed, "our work begun, continued, and ended in you." Everything has a life cycle, with a beginning, a middle, and an end—even congregations. Just like our human lives, institutions do not last forever. We didn't pray that morning that God would keep St. Peter's going forever, but only that we would glorify God through whatever we faced. At our best, we trusted that somehow God would be glorified in our endings, just as earlier building projects, the bursting enrollments in Sunday school, and a packed sanctuary on Easter pointed to God's glory in our beginnings and continued middles.

The day began with each congregation circling up with its own members. Playfulness and creativity made space for us to clarify our values and commitments, and to get to know each other. Each congregational group was asked to imagine and then act out a creature that would tell the "who and the why" of our communities. Congregational groups huddled around tables and brainstormed ideas for creatures. At the end of this time, we awkwardly embodied them like big communal puppets.

1 Buechner, *Whistling in the Dark*, 93–94.

2 Evangelical Lutheran Church in America, *Lutheran Book of Worship*, 49

The group of people from the church up in the Watchung Mountains, just north of us, huddled together, and then some people stretched out like enormous wings, and others in the middle as the body. They clumsily pretended to fly together around the Fellowship Hall. Like an albatross, they might seem ungainly, but they had a lot to share. The challenge was getting off the ground, but they trusted the Holy Spirit to move them.

Next, the members of St. Stephen, my husband's church just south of us, formed a circle with a central person in the middle, with others facing out, stretching and waving their arms around them. They described themselves as an octopus. With a shared purpose but many tasks, they were one body with many arms, each with different functions.

We couldn't decide on an actual creature to describe St. Peter's. After brainstorming animals like a koala or a St. Bernard, we decided an imaginary being best described us. We acted out a creature with big hands for serving, big ears for listening, big mouths that communicate well and often, all sustained by a big heart for loyalty and faith.

After lunch, we put up butcher paper and filled it with Post-its about ministry and mission, challenges and hopes. As the day progressed, it became evident that, despite being in the same denomination and region, we were very different communities. Any movement together would mean significant compromises on everything from worship styles to stewardship practices. While we met some great people, the discovery of incongruity led to disappointment among some of our leaders at St. Peter's. Perhaps, if we had more time, the leaders of our congregations might have been more creative in sharing resources, staff, or facilities. But that wasn't to be. We had such hope that this could save us, but no partnerships emerged. Much to our disappointment, that group of congregational leaders never met together again. The first raven came back to us with nothing in its beak.

One neighboring congregation invited us to sell our building outright and meet in their space on Sunday afternoons. As two separate congregations in one space, we could hold onto our unique identities. We'd relinquish building and staff expenses. Perhaps this was a second bird sent out. Might this congregation's invitation be a sign that St. Peter's would have a new place to land?

As the leaders of St. Peter's discussed the offer, it didn't seem to make sense for the greater church, or for our concept of ministry. Why be two Lutheran churches in one building? Sure, we'd both be able to maintain our differences in worship style, community, and practices, but how was that a faithful use of our resources? We graciously declined their invitation. The second raven returned with nothing in its beak.

Our options were narrowing. The more conversations we had, the more we realized that our most faithful option would be to close our doors and end St. Peter's ministry. The limiting of options meant that our safe little boat might soon have to dock, and our beautiful menagerie of occupants disembark. We would have to see just what it meant to glorify God with our ending.

11

2009

Maundy Thursday

Now before the festival of the Passover, Jesus knew that his hour had come to depart from this world and go to the Father. Having loved his own who were in the world, he loved them to the end (John 13:1).

The Future Task Force expressed gratitude for the Regional Mission Gathering, but they were frustrated that no cooperative future came from those conversations. In our meeting soon afterward, heaviness settled over the room as we named aloud exactly what this meant. We would have to close our doors and end the ministry of St. Peter's. Months spent exploring all options to determine the best way forward could not avoid this verdict. Other paths proved unviable or simply did not align with our values.

The Task Force's next decision would be to determine which congregation would be our "receiving congregation." This church would assist us in our closing, receive our roster of members, and care for our homebound members. Someone suggested that St. Stephen's Lutheran Church might be a suitable option for us. I stayed quiet, given that my husband was the pastor of this nearby congregation. I knew firsthand that the people of St. Stephen's were hospitable and faithful, and I trusted that Clark and the congregation would receive them well.

Grace reminded some of us how St. Peter's helped St. Stephen's get off the ground as a congregation with an investment of people and money decades earlier. "It'd be like we were returning to a part of ourselves, like when parents move in with their children when they get too old to live alone. If St. Stephen's is interested, I like the idea of going to them. They came from us, and we'd be an asset returning something of ourselves to them." St. Stephen's was a healthy congregation that St. Peter's could further strengthen. "We've got a lot to offer," someone had said.

One of my mentors, who walked alongside me through this time of discernment, invited me to pay attention to my body as we navigated the big questions. "God speaks through our bodies," she said. "Notice how your body feels while having important conversations. It'll tell you what you can never quite articulate with words. Where did you feel light, alive, responsive, excited? Where do you feel heavy, turned in, or slow? Watch, too, how others respond."

A sense of openness came over me during that Task Force meeting. I felt space to breathe in my body that I hadn't felt for a long time. We were finding a way forward, even when it meant a lot of loss. A new freedom and energy arrived among us as we named of a possible new beginning that would emerge from our ending.

Now, was St. Stephen's the right place to receive us? How would we fit in? Most importantly, would they even want us?! We still lacked clarity, but we were making progress toward a destination. I had been praying to proceed as the way opened. And even though the river was pulling us in an utterly heartbreaking direction, somehow the clarity of new hope gave us courage.

In early spring, I met Gloria to discuss the logistics of Holy Week. As the head of the Altar Guild, she helped coordinate details for worship on these most important days. She made sure all the banners were ready, the palms ordered, and the paraments pressed and ready to go. As we discussed each service, I realized it would likely be our last Holy Week together in the much-loved sanctuary. While our denomination gives rubrics for these Holy Days, every congregation celebrates them in their own unique ways. The rituals of these days convey the same story, but their expressions evolve in distinct ways over time. In our planning, we wanted to ensure that we didn't forget any revered customs and that the congregation's traditions would be honored.

The Triduum, or the "Three Days," begins with Maundy Thursday, where we remember the Last Supper and Jesus washing his disciples' feet. Jesus tells his friends that the one thing we must do is to love one another, as we have been loved. Jesus embodies this mandate (from which we get the Maundy, the name for this day) by washing his friends' feet and giving his life.

I preached that Maundy Thursday night about this love that would sustain us. Jesus washed feet and turned to the cross, loving his people through whatever ends they would face. I invited those present for worship that night to enter the story again and find hope and courage in it. When I was done preaching, the choir sang, and the congregation sat down in silence.

James, a shy and smiling middle school kid and our acolyte that night, picked up the brass candle lighter. Using the bell-shaped snuffer at the end, he slowly extinguished the candles. It took a while. First, he snuffed out the light of the two candles on the altar in their brass candlesticks, then the ten on the back wall altar. There were five candles on each side, set in arrow-shaped candelabras. James took his time. Despite his youth, he understood the solemnity of the night.

As the space got a little darker, I walked up the few steps of our raised pulpit. I picked up the purple brocade cloth, which was heavy with embroidery and golden fringe. Gloria had already walked to the front and waited at the top of the aisle to receive it. She took the cloth with tenderness and looked right at me. We both stood, still and silent, acknowledging what we were doing, all that it meant for us. We were beginning to clear the altar of all the things we used for worship, a ritual repeated every Maundy Thursday. Every year on that night, we strip the altar to symbolize the way Jesus was abandoned, stripped, and laid bare. Holding the brocade purple fabric, we silently recognized what the whole congregation also knew. The next time we would remove items from this sanctuary, it would be to give them away at our ending.

Gloria turned and, with the reverence she always gave to holy things of worship, carried it into the sacristy. I moved to the lectern, removed the matching purple brocade cloth, and handed it to Nancy, who helped with the Altar Guild and volunteered to participate in this ritual.

But as I walked to her, something happened that Gloria and I hadn't planned. A line of people stood in the center aisle, queued up just like they did to receive communion. Everyone wanted to be a part of this, not just the ones we'd asked to help. They, too, realized the significance of our last Maundy Thursday and felt drawn to participate in this holy act.

I had a moment of panic. Gloria and I had crafted a precise list of objects and the order in which they would be removed from the altar. However, I wanted everyone who stood in that line to be able to participate in this moment. So, like a baker who realized she needed to cut smaller pieces of cake to feed more people than initially planned, I quickly rationed the items in our space.

I took the black cardboard numbers from the wooden hymn board. But instead of pulling them all out and giving them out in one stack, I took just a few and gave them to the two children standing in line. In small stacks, I placed the hymn numbers in those little hands, those big hearts, who couldn't hold too much, but were eager to help be a part of this shared emptying.

Preacher and theologian Richard Lischer connects the stripping of the altar on Maundy Thursday with the art of losing.

> In a church that's filled with people who are being reduced in a hundred different ways—by illness, death, grief, betrayal, depression, and economic reversal, whose insurance has lapsed and whose dreams have been foreclosed—Holy Week teaches us all a lesson in losing. We are not losers, but we have been reduced, some of us to what feels like our touchstone. On Maundy Thursday, we discover that even when everything has been taken away, something remains.[1]

Everything disappeared from the front of the sanctuary. The offering plates, my purple stole, the big red altar book, the heavy brass altar stand, the cloths, both white and purple, on the altar, and then finally those brass candlesticks and candelabras. We practiced the art of losing, and in doing so, embodied the truth that even as we lost so much, something bigger remained. We had a Savior who knew the pain of loss and would carry us through—this One who would remain, no matter what. He would love us to the end.

1. Lischer, *Stripped Bare*, 12.

12

Eastertide 2009

But We Had Hoped

He asked them, "What things?" They replied, "The things about Jesus of Nazareth, who was a prophet mighty in deed and word before God and all the people, and how our chief priests and leaders handed him over to be condemned to death and crucified him. But we had hoped that he was the one to redeem Israel. (Luke 24:19–21).

A few days later, I returned to the sanctuary early on Sunday morning to prepare for Easter worship. Gloria and her team had spent Saturday putting back the candelabras and draping white brocade and embroidered cloths over the pulpit, lectern, and altar. Flowers were everywhere, mostly lilies with their aroma of resurrection. That spring, the congregation held onto the promises of Easter even as heartache over their future sat beneath the surface. We ate together and sang our alleluias. For a while, we let ourselves be held by the joy that does not depend on circumstance.

Celebrating the central story of our faith, that Christ conquered the power of death, gave us courage to claim bits of joy that spring. It wasn't because all the problems had disappeared, but because we needed to hear about how nothing at all, not even the end of our church, could separate us from God's love. The people of St. Peter's were adjusting to what we would soon lose and, perhaps because of that, weren't afraid to claim some honest Christian hope as well.

We needed such hope. The fragrance of the lilies and a few reverberating alleluias still hung in the air of the church as the Future Task Force reconvened. The primary task during Eastertide was to engage in conversations with members of the congregation, share the overarching plan, and listen to every kind of feedback. One member of the Task Force suggested that we invite members to write and share what they were thinking about and praying about. The hope was that, by writing, people could sort through the range of their feelings. These letters and conversations would create space for the whole community to acknowledge the emotions they were experiencing, along with the memories, worries, conflicts, or joys that were inevitably bound to accompany the difficult decisions ahead.

I thought then, and it still comes to mind now, of the children's book "Going on a Bear Hunt." The book tells the story of a family going on a bear hunt. The family on the hunt faces many obstacles that could deter them, but they forge through them. They come upon a raging river, and they say, "Oh no!! A river. A deep, cold river. We can't go over it. We can't go under it. We've got to go through it!"[1] This exact phrase happens repeatedly as the family faces mud, a snowstorm, and more before discovering the bear in a cave. "We can't go over it. We can't go under it! We've got to go through it." Each time the family faces some impediment that could stop them, they persevere through the challenge.

Much of the same apprehension often occurs with respect to grief, and all the sorrow, anger, fear, and regret that accompany it. We attempt to go around the disappointment we experience when outcomes we hope for don't happen. We may try to go over our grief or sorrow by burying it in busyness or simply ignoring it. Sometimes we duck under the complex emotions that we'd like to pretend aren't really there. Yet the only way to the other side, as we often learn the hard way, is through those rough conditions.

Our congregation didn't face rivers, mud, or snowstorms, but we faced obstacles just as murky and powerful. The impediments that St. Peter's faced weren't going to disappear. We could not go over the obstacles, or under them, or around them. We simply had to go through them. That communal resolve would be the only way to the other side, to a place of reconciliation, wholeness, and healing.

1. Rosen, *Going on a Bar Hunt*.

Some of our St. Peter's people responded with letters that were distributed more widely that spring. I wish we had received a greater response, but we were a small enough community that people felt heard in other ways, through conversations, attending our town hall meetings, or worshipping together. Each person found their own way through the complexity of feelings involved with closing their congregation.

We did receive a few letters. One couple, who had long been active at St. Peter's before moving to Pennsylvania, wrote a beautiful remembrance. Jim had spearheaded the annual Spaghetti Dinner and Variety Show, bringing humorous emcee energy to every interaction. I found his words touching. "St. Peter's is so much more than a building; it is a tight-knit family of people who have come together over the years to hear the word of God and share it with others in the community through words and deeds. And, that we can all still do anywhere, anytime, and anyplace."

Grace wrote pages and pages of reflection that included these words:

> Yes, I feel devastated deep down about the thought of St. Peter's, 'my church', closing, since I'm a lifetime member. I know a church is just a building, but one I've seen grow in my lifetime.
>
> I will always cherish all these wonderful memories, and I pray that wherever we are guided, we will feel comfortable, happy, and inspired by our new church family and minister. I wanted to be buried from St. Peter's, but is that crucial, as I'll be buried from another one of God's homes? I am willing to be positive and happy with new surroundings and come to feel a significant part of my new church family.

And then there was a letter from Amy. Amy and her husband had long been active at St. Peter's, raising their two college-aged daughters at church. Amy had served in every kind of leadership position. With quiet strength, she was the kind of person who brings insight to conversations because of her keen listening and observational skills.

The conflict over the years had hurt Amy, but she remained active and committed to the ministry of St. Peter's. Her persistence, faithfulness, and care for the people around her repeatedly inspired me. In her response to the questions we asked, she wrote:

> In the latest installment of the "Friendly Messenger," we have been asked to share in an "offering of letters' to express our feelings and thoughts on the pending closure of St. Peter's. I read with interest

> the list of suggested questions, but I did not see the question that I would have asked, which is "What makes me so disappointed?"
>
> "What makes me so disappointed?" That question is a very big and personal one for me. I would have to answer that while there was still time for a real turnaround at St. Peter's, all of our best evangelism efforts fell on deaf ears!
>
> As both a former member of and head of the St. Peter's Evangelism Committee, I can only feel a deep sense of personal and corporate disappointment that all the efforts that were expended by a small number of very dedicated individuals to encourage personal and individual invitation failed in the end, bringing us to the brink of the decision that we now face. The closure of St. Peter's will be a very sad and painful thing for me to witness.

"What makes you disappointed?" That was indeed a heavy question that I'm sure others were pondering, even if not articulating. Amy's words didn't seem too different from those of Jesus' disciples who, on the first Easter day, walked despondently down a dusty road. They hadn't yet seen the risen Christ and couldn't make sense of the news a few women had shared about finding the tomb empty. So, they walked along devastated, confused, and discouraged.

When the resurrected Jesus stepped in to walk beside them, they didn't yet recognize him. He asked them what they were visiting about, so they shared the latest news with this stranger. "We had hoped that this one was the one to redeem Israel," they began. We had hoped. Such utter disappointment in those three words. What these followers of Jesus longed for, hoped for, expected, believed in, invested in, gave their lives for—didn't happen. "We had hoped." That feeling of those two on the road to Emmaus is such a human one, the feeling of hopes dashed, expectations ruined, and visions of a bright future erased, shifted, or blurred.

Jesus met those two right in the center of their sadness, a reminder that the promise of Easter is never just jubilant joy; it's also trusting Jesus to show up in our disappointments. Jesus spent time talking with these mystified disciples, explaining in detail how he and his story linked back to all those stories in scripture. He wove their personal experience into the larger story of God's saving grace. Once they reached Emmaus, the two disciples pleaded with this stranger to stay with them a little bit longer. And there, around a kitchen table, Jesus took some bread and blessed it. Scripture tells us that the disciples' hearts burned within them, and they suddenly recognized Jesus. It was the ritual familiarity of a meal they had just eaten with Jesus a few days earlier. They recalled the assurance that accompanies the bread and wine from his hand: "Do this to remember me, in remembrance of me."

At St. Peter's, we were unmistakably a heartbroken and disappointed bunch in those days. Amy put the reality of these feelings into words, as she could do so well. Over the years, members of St. Peter's had made dozens of felt banners for worship. *We had hoped* could well have been our next felt banner project. If only we were creating new ones instead of trying to find homes for the ones we already had.

That spring, Amy pulled me aside one Sunday after having assisted me with serving the communion meal. She expressed again the hardship of facing our ending and dying. But she also said that, somehow, in our shared commitment to mutual discernment, a loosening of her anger was happening within her. With the reverence of someone who had experienced a miracle, Amy spoke of giving the wine to one of the individuals with whom she'd had the most conflict. As she served him, she felt an alleviating release of anger. The resentment was gone. She couldn't exactly explain it, but felt a wave of forgiveness, a peace, and healing flow through her.

We can't go over it. We can't go under it. We can only go through it. As Christian people, we get to trust that Jesus is walking alongside us. We're also given the company of others, as Amy would testify, who teach us all kinds of ways to live with forgiveness and hope. And, maybe, in the breaking of the bread and sharing the cup, we'll find our own hearts burning within us, too.

13

Spring 2009

Psalm 23

The Lord is my shepherd; I shall not want.
He makes me lie down in green pastures;
He leads me beside still waters;
He restores my soul (Psalm 23:1–3).

Now that our many options had been narrowed down to one, the Future Task Force began to shift its work. We focused intently on three main goals: 1) supporting the congregation in making the decision to end our ministry, 2) working with the council to prepare an actual resolution, and 3) figuring out what we needed to do once this decision was made.

Looking back on the document that outlined these tasks, I now see the vivid character of this congregation shining through it. One that grid, each of the main goals was listed, followed by all the tasks needed to accomplish them. Underneath every goal, the first task was prayer. "Pray: Encourage it among others. Do it ourselves." If our work wasn't to be grounded in God's presence, that utter confidence that God indeed accompanies us, we would truly be lost. That phrase: "Pray: Encourage it among others. Do it ourselves" echoed throughout the document and the hearts of the team.

When the Future Task Force shared their Bible stories at that first meeting, Gloria sat at the table, too. Gloria had been a member of St. Peter's for decades, since her marriage to George. She spent much of her childhood overseas and had a sharp mind with a deep well of faith. She said, "I think of Psalm 23. God will guide our paths."

This familiar psalm named our realities. For months, the Task Force had been discerning God's will for us. But that spring, they claimed a new role: they would shepherd the congregation, walking beside their brothers and sisters, guiding them along. We would share, listen, and communicate in every possible way to ensure the congregation would not resist our shared decision as we moved forward. As part of this work, I committed to visiting every household in the congregation. Not only did everyone need to know the process of what had happened and what would happen, but they also needed their pastor to accompany them—to name the truth that God would never leave their side, even through the valley of the shadow of death.

While the parishioners I visited had read updates and had a general understanding of what was happening, it was up to me to speak the very truth they most feared. My one-sentence spiel may be in my head forever: "After lots of conversations and a thorough exploration of other options, we're moving toward making the decision to conclude the ministry of St. Peter's."

The first few times this rolled off my lips, I'd choke up, almost as if I didn't want to believe it myself. I've heard bereaved people with similar shaky voices when they've had to announce that "my husband died" or "I now have only two daughters, our son passed away." Even our language, "passed away" or "no longer here," tries to remove the pain of saying out loud what is true that we can't quite believe, nor want to be true. And yet, people die. Success stories end. And institutions sometimes must close their doors.

In serving weak coffee and trays of packaged cookies, my hosts seemed to want to soften the blow of that sentence of mine that they probably dreaded was coming. Nobody seemed particularly surprised by my announcement, given our steady stream of communication updates. They were just sad. Nearly everybody asked if we had tried everything and if there were other options available to us.

As they talked and listened, the conversation eventually shifted to recalling all the ways God had blessed them through St. Peter's. More than I think I realized at the time, the sadder portions of many of these home conversations felt like a modern iteration of the ancient psalms of lament. They begin with big feelings. The psalmist names all that has gone wrong for them. "Out of the depths, I cry to you, O Lord!" (Ps. 130) and "My tears have been my food, day and night" (Ps. 42). But these psalms, full of anguish, anger, and despair, make this turn at the end. They conclude with words of deep faith and hope, Psalm 42 ends, "I hope in God; for I shall again praise the Lord, my help and my God." And Psalm 22, which begins, "my God, my God, why have you forsaken me!" shifts in tone as the psalmist says, "but all the nations of the world will praise your name."

Walter Brueggeman uses trajectory language to describe these lament psalms as moving from disorientation to reorientation. They begin with despair and then turn to name a sense of renewed wholeness.[1] I observed a similar shift in my conversations with St. Peter's people. First came the lament, naming their anger at this situation that was not as it should be, which wronged us. It was necessary to speak out loud their disappointments, anger, and frustration; to count their losses and display their grief. People need to start by communicating the honest truths of their hearts, trusting that someone has borne witness to them. Only then can they make that little turn to say, "But yet, God is faithful. And even so, God will care for me. Still, blessings remain." In so many of my conversations with people, this subtle shift happened. I tried to make space for lament, where people felt free to express their disorientation. Then, together, we were led to reorientation.

Those few weeks were some of the hardest I have ever experienced in ministry, but they demonstrated how much the church means to people and how congregations matter in personal lives. There would be no sense of loss if there had never been goodness. My people needed a place to share those heartbreaks, a person to bear witness to them, and I will forever be grateful for that privilege, even as it left me often weary and full of guilt, a sense of failure that I had somehow let them down. I was angry, too. Like the psalmist, I shook my fist at God, wondering why this was happening to me, to the people I loved. I found that all those feelings metabolized as tears—tears of anger, of sadness, of shame. The tears of anger were the worst, making me feel weak and vulnerable when I most wanted to be strong.

Thankfully, I had been given my own shepherd that year—a big black dog named Abbey. My sister-in-law had received a Fulbright scholarship, which allowed her and my brother to spend a year in southern India while she worked on her doctoral dissertation. They left their gentle and playful dog in our care, a big, black, border collie-husky mix they'd rescued and who, in many ways, rescued me.

1. Brueggemann, *Spirituality of the Psalms*, 11.

Most days, I came home carrying with me the grief of this community that was losing so much. I put on my walking shoes, got Abbey on a leash, and began walking. Putting one foot in front of the other, surrounded by the big trees of central New Jersey, a happy dog by my side, I metabolized the sadness, anger, and guilt I felt. A Latin proverb, *solvitar ambulando,* means "it is solved by walking." A good walk can help sort out all kinds of feelings and problems when we get stuck. Moving helps us think more clearly and get creative. I often thought of that 23rd Psalm on these walks, not only because I walked around a lake in the town we lived in, our own still waters. It was also those words, "He restores my soul." Those walks with God and Abbey were restorative for me.

But Abbey wasn't just a good walker; she was a herder. Abbey had never met a sheep, but this instinct to herd was a part of her. We lived in the parsonage of the church my husband served, a 1960s split-level home with five floors and numerous steps. Whenever Clark and I were on separate floors, Abbey would circle around us, attempting to get us closer, until she finally gave up and sat on the landing. She wouldn't eat unless we were all together.

Spending those months being herded by Abbey, I came to understand a deeper truth about our Good Shepherd. God is bound and determined to keep God's people together. Sheep, after all, don't survive well on their own. They aren't like those solitary wolves who can lurk about alone. For sheep, their strength is in their flock. Protection is found in community. The same is true for us Christians.

We need a flock because there will come a time when our prayers feel empty and the voices of doubt become too loud. On our own, our vision of God gets small, and our despair can become enormous. We get stuck in our disorientation. We need a flock because, as Abbey reminded me, it just gets lonely to eat by ourselves.

The people of St. Peter's knew how to be a flock. They knew how to show up for people through prayers, visits, food, and parties. They were also deeply committed to ensuring that the entire flock could participate in making decisions together. So, while I talked with each of our members, our leaders did the same. They knocked on doors and made phone calls, sitting down over cups of coffee with their sadness and offers of support as others lamented and hoped. They did their own grieving and processing, but also cared for others in their struggles. We were herded, held together.

Meanwhile, the leaders worked with our partners in the Office of the Bishop to compile all the necessary resolutions for the congregational vote. The Future Task Force handed over their work to the Council, who made their own small changes to the proposals, resolutions, and plans. We worked toward a congregational meeting at the beginning of June, when we herded our people together for the final vote.

That day finally came. On Holy Trinity Sunday, we worshipped with more people in the sanctuary than we had seen for months. Following the dismissal, "Go in peace. Serve the Lord," the congregation made their way to the Fellowship Hall for a potluck lunch before the meeting. After changing out of my worship attire, but not entirely ready to address the congregation in the critical meeting before us, I headed to the kitchen to talk with the people preparing food.

The kitchen at St. Peter's was full of light. Oversized windows let in sun from the east, and white cupboards held the treasures of a church kitchen. Yellowed tape held a chart on one of the cupboards, which showed the measurement of coffee grounds needed for the enormous percolator. In one cupboard sat a big old cookie tin where we kept the sugar. Someone joked that it was our own miracle, like the widow's oil and grain that fed Elijah through the drought. No one ever saw someone adding to it, but it always had plenty of sugar to sweeten our coffee. That bin was never empty.

I stood in the kitchen as a small group of our people set out the napkins and plates. One woman had the large metallic coffee pot and was filling it with water, while another was placing the filter into the basket at the top of the percolator and, without referencing the guide, scooping just the right amount of coffee grounds into it. Like a pit crew at a car race, they worked together with ease and familiarity. They had been doing this together for decades.

Just like that feast prepared in Psalm 23, on that June day, we had our own feast. (And, given the conflict that had been a part of the congregation my whole tenure and before it, I'm sure some of them felt as if it was about to be served and eaten in the presence of enemies.) Over the years, St. Peter's had built a tradition of having a potluck meal before any congregational meeting. Eating together helps solidify connections before jumping into business, especially the hard conversations. Most importantly, one should never make a big decision on an empty stomach.

I stood by the serving window that day, talking with those busy preparing the meal. Our team had completed its work. The reports were compiled, and the drafts of our proposals had been prepared and okayed by the Office of the Bishop. Everyone knew the stakes of what lay ahead. In the meantime, we'd eat and we'd laugh. This was a time to enjoy the goodness of our flock.

Because it was a small enough community, St. Peter's had a sort of informal organization about who would bring various dishes to a potluck. Grace would always bring her ham salad sandwiches. Katherine would bring pasta e fagioli. Ethel had incredible rice pudding. Amy made brownies. I simply brought my anxiety.

I hadn't slept well for weeks. The same was surely true for Katherine and other leaders. The grief and the loss our people were experiencing weighed heavily on me. But I had deep confidence that we were being led on the right path, for Christ's name's sake. Enough conversation had taken place to indicate this was absolutely the right decision, even if it was hard.

I have heard similar heartbreaking resignation elsewhere, especially in instances of parishioners making end-of-life decisions. These dear people had gone through chemotherapy, and despite undergoing all of the recommended treatment, nevertheless faced a ferocious return of the cancer. With sadness and courage, they would say, "I'm ready to be done. I'm weary. I want to make the most of whatever time I have left." Or others who receive a devastating diagnosis, and say, "I'm 86 and lived a good life. I'd rather call hospice than go through all that treatment."

Not everyone reaches this level of clarity in life and death moments. Many can't or don't want to make that same decision. But for those who do, it is radically liberating to allow death to take its course. It's freeing not just for the people who choose palliative care or to stop all the extraordinary life-continuing measures, but it can be equally liberating for those who love them. Many people, though never enough, make their wishes clear in a living will. Whatever a doctor may recommend be done, it is ultimately up to the patient and her closest companions to decide on courageous steps that lead toward dying.

My Dad claimed the same bold clarity about his dying as he had with big decisions in his life. In June, just before his 51st birthday, he was diagnosed with Multiple Myeloma, a blood disease. We had hoped that after a few rounds of chemotherapy, he would have a bone marrow transplant and be given years more to live. But by October, his kidneys had failed, and his GI system stopped working. His bones ached unbearably as the cancer spread relentlessly in his body. Dad spent weeks, lonely and painful weeks, in the hospital. So, he talked with my Mom and his doctor. He called me and my brother home. He was ready to stop all treatment. After receiving one last round of dialysis, we would take him home to his favorite chair and his own bed to die, with family surrounding him in love.

My dad kept a blog about pastoral leadership and faith. Once he had made the decision to suspend all further treatment, he wanted to write one last post. I volunteered to be the one with a pad of paper and a pen in hand, there in the dialysis center, to serve as the scribe for his dictation. As I sat next to him and took down his words, a nurse brought Dad a blanket, fresh from the warmer, and gently put it on his lap. Seeing me, she returned with another blanket and tucked me into the warmth, too.

I wrote as my dad dictated words that he had been ruminating on for hours, if not days. "We have decided to return home to our house on Freedom Drive to begin hospice. The doctors indicate that the clock running correctly will offer me days and weeks, but not likely months or more. There is no exact time, but there is a promise . . . Now I wait for a promise that is sure and true. Nothing can separate us . . . In the coming days I will pray again and again what I prayed at the beginning of this journey. 'May God grant us a quiet night, and peace at the last.'"[2]

My father was able to make that decision because he trusted in a promise of something more. He leaned into the hope of love from which we can never be separated, of peace at the last, of life beyond death.

The same conviction held our little community in New Jersey. Our people trusted that there was a future beyond the ending, new life on the other side of the closing. After months of prayer, study, and conversation, and despite some anger, arguments, and mistakes along the way, they came to this decision together, communally. The best choice, the most faithful one, would be to end their ministry. They chose to allow the congregation to die. While we had the support and care of the Office of the Bishop, this was never the decision of that office. It wasn't mine either. The congregation was ready to do the hard thing.

The ham salad and brownies of that day were what they always were—homemade, delicious, and plentiful. We did what we always did: we ate them with gratitude. And then we engaged another ritual of thanks that accompanied every potluck: we sang.

> Bind us together, Lord, Bind us together,
> With cords that cannot be broken.
> Bind us together, Lord, Bind us together,
> Bind us together in love.[3]

2. Olson, *Notes to Eli*, 129.

3. Evangelical Lutheran Church in America, *Evangelical Lutheran Worship*, 748.

We sang together, in part because this community loved to sing. But it's also a leadership hack I learned from my godfather, Brian. When we're anxious, our hearts race, our minds don't think well, and our breathing gets out of whack. We start living in our "reptile brain," panicking, ready to fight, flee, or freeze. But singing slows our breathing, regulates our nervous system, and helps us think more clearly. We sang that Sunday afternoon so that we could experience in our bodies the truth that, despite all our differences and sometimes our discord, we were one congregation. As we sang, the Spirit bound us together. It was yet another way that this flock of ours could be restored, ready to step into the valley of the shadow of death.

Katherine called the meeting to order. She shared the process and work of the Future Task Force, described our financial challenges, and outlined our congregation's dwindling capacity to carry out the ministry of being church. She answered questions, though there weren't many. And then, with her voice cracking and tears in her eyes, Katherine read aloud the first of the resolutions, which would be approved, not unanimously but by a good majority of the congregation casting ballots.

> Be it resolved that:
> We, the members of St. Peter's Evangelical Lutheran Church, declare our intention to discontinue our ministry and to subsequently dissolve the congregation in North Plainfield, New Jersey. After extensive and prayerful deliberation, we are saddened to cast our votes for discontinuance and dissolution. The changing context of our ministry and the diminished human and financial resources available to us make it extremely difficult to conduct a sustainable ministry in this location.

14

June 2009

Paul's Churches (the churches Paul served)

I pray that Christ may dwell in your hearts through faith, as you are being rooted and grounded in love. I pray that you may have the power to comprehend, with all the saints, what is the breadth and length and height and depth, and to know the love of Christ that surpasses knowledge, so that you may be filled with all the fullness of God. Now to him who by the power at work within us is able to accomplish abundantly far more than all we can ask or imagine, to him be glory in the church and in Christ Jesus to all generations, forever and ever (Ephesians 3:14–21).

Despite a childhood immersed in church and Bible stories, I didn't learn until college that a large portion of the New Testament consisted of what is basically pastoral correspondence. No one outside of church circles uses the word "epistle" to speak of letters. Discovering that these books of the New Testament didn't drop from heaven, but were once actual letters written to particular communities, for particular occasions, by particular evangelists, gave me a new understanding. What was once ancient mail came to serve as sacred texts for billions of people. Their holiness is evident in the way they still speak to us, carry meaning, and offer direction despite centuries and vast cultural differences between us.

While God did not write the Bible with a divine pen, our scripture still bears God's fingerprints through the people who compiled it. Paul (or one of his close friends, whom I like to call "faux-Paul") wrote that "all scripture is inspired by God" (2 Tim. 3:16). The word so often translated in English as "inspired" is a term Paul coined: *theopnuestos*. It's a compound Greek word, *theo* (God) and *pneo* (to exhale, breathe out, blow like wind). In creating this word, Paul describes how our sacred text is a living, breathing word. The words are inspired (the Spirit in them), not because God wrote them word for word with a giant, holy hand, but because they bear the breath of God.[1] They exhale God's life into us, like an EMT breathes into a stranger to revive them while doing CPR. In scripture, we read centuries-old words that continue to infuse God's message into us.

In worship that summer, thanks to the blessings of the lectionary, we read (faux) Paul's words to the community in Ephesus. This "book" began as a letter that names God's generosity and grace to a community divided and in conflict. With a pastoral heart and some instruction, the letter declares that God's lavish love transforms how we act toward one another and in the world. Even in prison, Paul anchored his faith, courage, and hope in Jesus.

The words of Ephesians were words our community needed to hear that summer. We soaked up gratitude for one another, "I do not cease to give thanks for you" (Eph. 1:16). Personally, I tried to anchor my leadership in his pastoral prayer, inviting us to be rooted and grounded in the full three-dimensional power of God's love. "The breadth and length and heighth and depth." Mostly, I needed to know that God would be able to accomplish in us far more than I could ever imagine or ask. (Eph. 3:14–21).

In the days after the congregation registered their historic vote to end the ministry of St. Peter's, Katherine and I decided to follow Paul in a most literal sense. We wrote letters. Every household received letters informing them of what they already knew: thirty-one people gathered on a Sunday in June and voted to end the ministry of St. Peter's Lutheran Church. Like Paul, we began with gratitude for the Future Task Force, whose work was now done. The letter outlined details of how our closing would unfold in the coming months. Katherine ended with the words, "All of our hearts are heavy. May we look to God so that we can close with hope . . . and continue St. Peter's ministry in another place."

After we sent all those letters to members, friends, and neighbors, we got to work. First, we needed to fill out the rosters of the committees that

1. Held-Evans, *Inspired*, xxiii.

would prepare for our end. To cover all the tasks with a limited bench of players, we moved people around, inviting members into various roles and leadership positions that they hadn't previously considered. We tapped Jill to fill in on the council for someone who had taken leadership in another committee. Every other time we'd asked Jill for this kind of leadership role, she declined. Jill was in her mid-fifties and had recently and suddenly been widowed. She had the biggest heart for service and would happily drop what she was doing to help anyone, but she never believed herself capable of leadership. But she said yes because she knew we needed all hands on deck. Jill's presence and insights turned out to be just what we needed. Underestimating untapped gifts waiting to be unleashed, she discovered strength in herself that she didn't know existed.

The building sale team met with realtors and began the process of listing the church building for sale. But, given that we were months away from actually closing the doors, nobody felt ready to put up a "For Sale" sign outside. Still, we put it on the market. The congregation repeatedly expressed a desire for the building to remain a church that another faith community could use for worship. I worried we'd eventually have to let this dream go, but I, too, hoped for a faithful future for the space that formed us.

Another team began to review all the papers, collecting important documents that would be held in the care of our denomination's archive center at our seminary in Philadelphia. We sorted through boxes of files, shredding old financial records. Minutes from the Ladies' Missionary Society meetings, written in beautifully embellished cursive, had to go. Grace, George, and others helped us learn some of the stories behind the sepia photographs with captions in fancy script—stories of saints who had given so much to the congregation.

The church had closets and cupboards full of what many people might consider junk, but had once been necessary for ministry. Our people dug through dusty boxes and piles of books, revealing a rich history of curriculum changes and adaptations to faith formation programming over the last century. We skimmed and discarded or recycled old Sunday School books, lesson plans, and assorted Bible Studies. Pageant props and sets from the annual variety show took us back in time. This team of treasure hunters faithfully sorted out what was worth saving or sharing, and what needed to be tossed.

Soon, our Fellowship Hall became a combination yard sale and museum. We set out all the items that were still usable and appreciated, for

St. Peter's people to claim and take for their own memories or use. After our people claimed their treasures, we invited neighboring congregations to visit and see if they could use anything for their ministries.

Some things were too precious to put on those tables. The communion vessels, fabrics, and other worship items were numbered among these treasures. We believed they had value beyond merely our memories. Our people didn't want them to go to waste or sit on a shelf somewhere. They hoped that others could use them for their intended purpose in the worship life of another congregation. We catalogued these objects and began to share their availability with other faith communities.

As St. Peter's prepared to close its doors, another congregation thirty miles west of us was getting ready to open theirs. Living Waters Lutheran Church was about to move into their own building after years of worshiping in a local school. They needed some of what we had to share. I remember the Living Waters' pastor and leadership team walking through our space to consider items they might receive from us. They did this with respectful compassion, not like they were shopping on Black Friday or picking through a fire sale. They honored us and our history. Our piano landed at Living Waters. So did the plates, cups, mugs, silverware, and dishes from our kitchen—everything needed to set up a great cooking and serving place.

The items we used in worship were the hardest to give away. Our silver chalices, including a relatively new set given in Charlie's memory, were particularly precious to many of us. A fish etching in the metal pointed not only to Peter the fisherman, but to the meals of fish Jesus ate, whether it was with lunch for thousands in a field or a resurrection breakfast on the beach one morning. To those in the world who don't know Christian worship, these polished vessels would've seemed mere metal objects. To us, they were doorways into grace. The sight and use of them drew us into the mystery of God's presence.

Gordon Lathrop describes the unique power of the material objects of our worship life:

> We do need some things. It seems as if we ought to be above such material crutches, as if a gathering to come together to speak of God ought to be more spiritual. But that is just the point: for the great Christian tradition, the spiritual is intimately involved with the material, the truth about God inseparable from the ordinary, as inseparable from God was from the humanity in Jesus. If these

> things be crutches, so be it. They will then be for us the very 'ford, bridge, door, ship and stretcher' that Luther said we need.[2]

Those holy things of St. Peter's acted as bridges, doors, and ships that connected us to God. They not only held the bread and wine of communion, but they also carried grace. Like crutches, they supported us every week as we stood before God. They pointed us to our saving story and bound us together as a community. Gloria and our people understood this and committed their energies to ensuring that these vessels of grace would continue to be used for their intended purpose.

When no one nearby seemed interested in these treasured "crutches," we started to look beyond New Jersey. I grew up in Denver, Colorado, and still had friends serving congregations there. I heard about a newly formed congregation committed to ancient liturgy and radical welcome, weaving new practices and old rituals together in a boldly inclusive and gracious manner. They had been worshiping in their pastor's living room, but in 2009, they found a home to worship and needed some of the holy things of worship.

The House for All Saints and Sinners was happy to receive our precious "crutches" to help them limp along in lives of grace. Our two-foot-tall brass altar cross with "INRI" embossed on it, matching brass candlesticks, the altar book stand, and some of our paraments were all going to be shipped to Denver. I felt such joy in being able to announce their creative reuse.

Our prayers for that new mission accompanied the objects we sent. But none of us could have guessed that this new congregation, The House for Saints and Sinners, would become known throughout the country as a leader in renewing worship, deep theological thinking, and radical welcome to those on the edges of faith, especially for queer folks. That congregation in Denver was a refuge and witness, and their pastor, Nadia Bolz-Weber, became a prominent theological thinker and speaker. In 2013, four years after our worship items were shipped to Denver, a Washington Post article showed Pastor Bolz-Weber presiding at communion. With her gracious presence, she stood behind our brass cross, her arms stretched in welcome next to the brass candlesticks that once stood on the altar where we had communed.[3]

When I saw that picture, my breath caught in my throat. Those candlesticks were given a new life. St. Peter's might have closed, but the

2. Lathrop, *Holy Things*, 90.

3. Boorstein, *Bolz-Weber*.

light of Christ had not died. The faith continued, and the church could not be stopped. It would take a different shape, be lived out in new ways, but new communities would share the same message of grace, be moved by the same commitment to serve, and ground their lives in the ancient prayers that still give life and hope to so many.

A man named Ted served on the Future Task Force. In their mid-fifties, Ted and his wife, Ingrid, were among our younger members. They sang in the choir and were deeply committed to service. Having raised their kids at St. Peter's, they recently became empty nesters. Ted had been able to avoid getting caught on either side of the conflict over the years. He expressed his faith more through service than testimony, and the love of singing in four-part harmony kept him connected to the church, even amid the doubts and assurances of his faith.

The night our Future Task Force discussed resonant Bible stories, Ted spoke about the early Christians who faced such persecution and overwhelming odds. Our local problems seemed minuscule in comparison. Ted thought that if the early church could persist through its challenges, we could endure through ours.

Writing to his people from prison, Paul knew that the Christian life was anything but easy. Being human, much less following a Savior who lived with radical self-giving, implied suffering. Despite Paul's own persecution, imprisonment, and struggle, he refused to cease witnessing for Christ's love. He kept encouraging his communities to remain faithful to love that is broad and wide, and to keep trusting that God would bless us beyond our imaginings.

The people of that community in Ephesus (and Corinth, Rome, Galatia, and Thessaloniki) did persist. Paul kept writing, teaching, and encouraging, until the Roman Empire beheaded him because of his faith in Jesus. Still, even after Paul was martyred, those communities continued to come together, hold material goods in common, pass on the faith, and share (and save) the treasured letters from their brother Paul. Today, however, if we were to travel to Ephesus, Thessaloniki, or Corinth, we wouldn't find those communities practicing their faith. They no longer exist.

Yet their faith persists. It continues beyond what they could have ever asked or imagined. Even though those churches are no longer, the Church remains. The body of Christ still lives, thriving, moving, serving, loving, proclaiming, advocating, persisting still—in all kinds of ways and places. Maybe not in the original church of Ephesus or at St. Peter's Lutheran

Church in North Plainfield. But the Church of Jesus Christ endures wherever followers of his gather.

Our namesake, Peter, advised many early followers of Jesus as they formed communities. Legend has it that when a missionary and a student of Peter's named Pancratius left on his missionary journeys, Peter filled his bags with items helpful for building worshiping communities. Eventually, Pancratius would become the Bishop of Taormina in Sicily. But when he was starting, Peter sent him with "two Gospel books, two books of Acts composed by the divine Apostle Paul, two sets of silver paten-and-chalice (*diskopoteria*), two crosses made of cedar boards, and two volumes (*tomoi*) of the divine picture stories (*Vita S. Pancratii*)."[4]

Peter's protégé journeyed with the stuff needed to carry the story and the grace of the church. He brought some of the very same objects we relied on in North Plainfield and later gave away in love. Through those objects and the witness of the people who used them, the churches in Philippi, Ephesus, or Corinth live on. The faith those early Christians embodied has not died. In fact, we might say that it's carried all over the world every day in chalices, books, and crosses. It's read in every copy of the New Testament. Generations of storytellers, singers, and worshippers pass it on. The church continues through the centuries with all it needs—holy things, faithful people, and the grace of God.

4. Lathrop, *Holy Things*, 88.

15

Summer 2009

Do Not Worry

[Jesus said,] "Therefore, I tell you, do not worry about your life, what you will eat or what you will drink, or about your body, what you will wear. Is not life more than food and the body more than clothing? Look at the birds of the air: they neither sow nor reap nor gather into barns, and yet your heavenly Father feeds them. Are you not of more value than they?" (Matthew 6:25–26).

Clara led from the margins with quiet and gentle strength, preferring to listen more than speak. When this St. Peter's saint talked, others listened gladly. We trusted her intrinsically. Clara grounded her life in scripture. She studied it for her own personal devotions and would never miss a chance to discuss scripture in community. During our Bible studies, she often had multiple Bibles with different translations lying on the table. When I took Sundays off for vacation, Clara would step in to lead worship and deliver the sermon. She likely would have become a pastor if she had been born a few decades later. But still, the Spirit found a way to use her and her gifts.

One Sunday, when we discussed the various stories of scripture that mirrored our life together at St. Peter's, Clara lifted some words from Jesus' Sermon on the Mount: "Do not worry about tomorrow, for tomorrow will bring worries of its own" (Mt. 6:34). Clara shared how, throughout all the unknowns, she held onto the truth that God would care for our tomorrows, which helped her be less anxious in her todays.

Clara knew something about living in challenging situations with a calm and steady spirit, unfazed by what might cause others anxiety. After serving as a nurse in hospitals and clinics all over the world for the military, she ended her career teaching nursing students. Through it all, she read the Bible. Clara knew it inside and out, pored over commentaries, various studies, and devotionals. This immersion in scripture gave her a foundation of faith, a commitment to service, and a deep care for others. By the time I met Clara, she was retired, her hair thick and white, but her body quick and stable like her mind.

In the months following our vote to close, my anxiety increased significantly, in part because of all that needed to be done with our building, but mostly because of our people. Clara, with her compassionate perceptiveness, would notice my worry, and she'd gently touch my arm, lean in, and say, "Don't worry, Pastor, remember the birds." I tried, but the needs of our people weighed on me. I especially worried about our homebound folks, who didn't stop needing care, companionship, and communion just because their church closed.

In my worry, I did what my pastor-friend Fred advised me to do: I made visits. It turns out that the task that most relieved my worry was to be with the very people about whom I worried. Just being with them helped diminish my anxiety. Maybe Jesus meant his words in the most literal of ways. *Do not worry. Look at the birds.* I'm not sure the birds are designed to be an object lesson, but we are to look at them. Observe them. Use their carefree existence as an invitation to be present and available to what is right in front of us now. Watch the birds. Smell the roses. Notice the physical world around you. Pay attention to the present moment, to the people you are with now. Don't miss out on today by worrying about tomorrow. Or, the lesson I took, "instead of worrying what will happen to your people tomorrow, be with them today."

On the days when I felt most anxious, when emails about real estate filled my inbox and the list of to-dos overwhelmed me, I left the office, hopped into my little mermaid green Toyota, and went to see my people. I traveled all over the place to see our homebound folks or those in nursing homes. It wasn't just that they needed support and would benefit from companionship. Their presence in my life pulled me out of my own spinning mind.

During these visits, we discussed where they wanted to transfer their membership. Many would connect with St. Stephen's, our designated receiving congregation. Others lived closer to other congregations or had personal connections with other pastors. I assured all of them that they would be cared for, prayed for, and visited.

One of my favorite visits was to Matilda, or Tillie as we knew her. She was one of those widows whose deep commitment makes the church work. In my early days, before her body began to fail her, Tillie was one of the first to arrive at church on Sunday mornings. She puttered around the kitchen, getting the coffee on. I often found Tillie sitting at the end of the stage in the Fellowship Hall on those Sunday mornings as everyone else got to church, legs dangling like a schoolgirl, chatting with her friends.

One January morning, Tillie fell on the ice and broke her hip. The days following such a mishap are never easy. For Tillie, they were uncharacteristically sad. She didn't know if she'd return to her independent living situation or, for that matter, what her future would look like. But when I visited her a week or two after surgery, she had settled into a nursing home for rehabilitation. I walked into her room, and she gave me the brightest smile. Tillie talked about how far she could walk down the hall with her walker, taking pride in her accomplishments. I commented on her total 180-degree shift in attitude and asked her what brought it about. She looked sort of embarrassed and said, "You'll never believe me."

"Try me," I said.

"Well, it's a cardinal," she said. "Every day, there's a cardinal outside my window. It's not there now. But it comes every day." And then, she said, "It makes me feel like I'm not alone. Like it's telling me that God's with me. Silly, I know, it's just a bird. But it gives me such hope."

My visits took me to Marie, who lived with dementia. I was lucky enough to have scheduled a visit with her just a few months before she died. The progression of her dementia was startling. Pulling up any words, much less the right words, was really tough for Marie. As I talked and prayed that afternoon, her daughter happened to drop in for a visit. A bright smile appeared on Marie's face when she saw the milkshake in her daughter's hand. When Marie took a sip through the straw, she closed her eyes, savoring it. I asked her what flavor of shake it was, and her forehead wrinkled as she tried to pull up the word. We waited a while, and finally she looked at me, proud to have found the word she was looking for, "happy." The shake was happy flavored.

As Marie's dementia progressed, her children hired a full-time caregiver, Wilma, to feed her, tend to her physical needs, and help her around her apartment. She took such loving care of Marie, reading scripture to her in her thick Bahamian accent and singing hymns with her. As Marie declined, I talked a lot with Wilma, whose faith had sustained her through many of life's challenges. When Marie was dying, I prayed, and Wilma would sing. Actually, we both prayed, Wilma's prayers were just much more melodic. She sang old gospel songs, *The Old Rugged Cross, In the Garden, Peace like a River.* And always, *His Eye is on the Sparrow.*

> Why should I feel discouraged?
> Why should the shadows come? . . .
> His eye is on the sparrow,
> And I know He watches me[1]

As we sang, her deep alto voice gave me solace. God watches the sparrow and would take care of our people. God had cared for them well before my time, and surely God would care for them into the future.

In many of my visits, people would share about my predecessor, Pastor Nelson. While some of our people had complicated relationships and conflicted history with him, Pastor Nelson was known for providing steady pastoral care for his people. He particularly knew how to be present for members who could not get to church. They shared how much he meant to them, how his showing up mattered. When he retired, he graciously handed those dear ones he loved over to God, the congregation, and me. In retrospect, I realize how difficult this loving relinquishment must have been. It demonstrated his trust in God and the church to continue caring for and keeping the people he served.

I had lunch with Pastor Nelson that summer before our closing. He spent decades as the pastor of St. Peter's, investing his whole self into that congregation. Pastor Nelson had been respectful of me during my time at St. Peter's, giving me space and never interfering. This is the expectation within our denomination, and I experienced the gift of those intentional boundaries. Despite living in town, he honored my role and his retirement, and I rarely saw him. He came to funerals, but never overstepped.

I owed it to him to discuss how we arrived at our current situation and the plans for what would follow after we closed. Over lunch at a local restaurant, he shared how devastated and angry he was that this was

1. Martin, *His Eye is On The Sparrow.*

happening to a place he loved so much, to a community to which he had given so much of himself. His time serving there wasn't always easy, but he cared for them. He, too, had much to grieve. But sometime in the conversation, I remember Pastor Nelson setting aside his anger and disappointment and asking about the well-being of our people.

In this pastoral moment, Pastor Nelson exposed his love for the congregation. He modeled for me what it means to consider the birds and know that our God, who cares for the sparrow, would care for each of us. As the church closed, I would soon need to entrust our people to God, in whose care they had always been, as Pastor Nelson did. I knew it wouldn't be easy, but I had to trust that, as God had done before, God would keep putting people into their lives who would provide them with support, care, and belonging.

I visited Hugh and Bertie. They were in their 90s and lived in a lovely little ranch house near the church. Hugh had fought multiple kinds of cancer for over a decade. Bertie's days were full. Not only did she care for Bob, sorting through piles and piles of insurance papers that covered their dining room table, but she also kept up with her kids and grandkids. She had a thousand jobs to do, and her list of worries dwarfed mine. But whenever I showed up at their house, Bertie would stop what she was doing and stand waiting at the door to greet me.

When I visited, Bertie set out a little lunch on a folding metal TV table, with an extra tray set up for communion. Hugh always had a bologna sandwich, and Bertie ate a small cup of yogurt. But without fail, Bertie made me a special sandwich. It had a filling of egg and shrimp salad piled between two slices of white bread. While I enjoy egg salad sandwiches, I'm not a fan of shrimp in any form. The first time I visited, in an attempt to be a gracious guest, I told her how delicious the shrimp-egg salad tasted. From then on, she made that sandwich just for me. I piled on pickles as a sort of chaser.

As we ate, the very busy and worried Bertie, who spent every moment caring for Hugh and everyone else in her orbit, sat on a simple wooden chair beside Hugh's recliner. She looked right at me and asked me how I was faring. I shared about all the developments at St. Peter's, the changes, and how they unfolded. I had my small communion kit in tow, containing a little bit of wine and some tiny wafers of bread, which Hugh and Bertie always received with such gratitude. We prayed together, which for me is shorthand for handing off life's worries to God.

Bertie always walked me to the door as I left, leaning out the storm door to ensure I was okay, waving until I pulled away from their little house. As I thought about all that she needed to do, I couldn't help but be amazed at the undivided attention she gave to me. Her worries never kept her eyes from being fully present. Every time I left their home, I felt grounded all over again. The people, yes, the people. Look at the lilies in the field. Look at the birds of the air.

Hugh died soon after St. Peter's closed. Bertie, unsurprisingly, lived to be 95. The photo in her obituary shows her standing at her front door, leaning out and smiling with an energetic thumbs-up. That's how I remember her in my own last glimpse of her years before. In her obituary, Bertie's family gave special thanks to her neighbors who helped her stay in her home to the end. They also expressed gratitude to her mailman, Eddie. I've read hundreds of obituaries, but only Bertie's gives gratitude to a mail carrier. It makes me want to meet this Eddie, who must've delivered a lot of joy to people on his route.

Reading that obituary years later felt like an answered prayer. I had worried so much about Bertie and the other members of St. Peter's. I prayed that people would show up for them, that they wouldn't be forgotten. God responded and blessed Bertie with, among other friends, a mail carrier who knew how to look out for her. His eye is on the sparrow, and I know God watched over her.

"Consider the birds," says Jesus. As Clara reminded me, birds are all we need to recall that the God who cares for us is never far off. The revelations of God's presence are seldom shiny and loud. Sometimes they're as simple as a red bird against the snow outside a nursing home window. Sometimes they're egg salad sandwiches with shrimp tucked in because someone thinks you matter. Sometimes they're as ordinary as a mailman who pays close attention to a widow along his route. Do not worry, but look at the birds, the lilies. God will not abandon us or the people we love. God's eye is on the sparrow.

16

August 2009

Planting Seeds

[Jesus said], "Very truly, I tell you, unless a grain of wheat falls into the earth and dies, it remains just a single grain, but if it dies it bears much fruit" (John 20:24).

In August, we discovered a large hole in one of our stained-glass windows. When Roy first told me one of our windows was broken, I thought someone must have thrown something or shot a hole through it. But it turned out to be the crucifixion window, which hung on an inside wall of the sanctuary. The window opened to a tiny interior courtyard in the center of the building. The damage couldn't have been intentionally done. People thought it might have been a rock that fell through the glass, but it seems impossible that a rock could have fallen with enough force through that window to cause the break. It remains a mystery.

The rock, or whatever it was, made a baseball-sized, jagged hole in the horizontal beam of the cross, just to the left of Jesus and his thorny crown, with cracks spread into the glass around it. The contrast between the deep brown stained glass and the light streaming through the opening made the appearance of that hole even more jarring. It's the last thing our little vulnerable community needed—a hole in the crucifixion window.

Many people had connections to those windows. Their family members, or they themselves, had generously contributed to the cost of their purchase. The names of loved ones were etched into the glass. With the uncertainty of what would happen to the building, they wanted to ensure that the windows would not be neglected or destroyed.

A few of our leaders even began investigating what it would take to remove the windows from the building to preserve them for our community. I struggled against this for a few reasons. First, the removal and installation of the windows elsewhere would be expensive, likely thousands of dollars. Second, we didn't know where they would go. While many St. Peter's members would affiliate with one congregation, we could not expect that our receiving congregation would have the architecture or resources to install our windows. Even with all these hurdles, some of our people still clung to the possibility that we could somehow keep them as our own.

As often happens, when so much is being lost, we try to hold onto something, anything. Those windows were more than just glass and pigment, more than ecclesiastical art. The windows held precious memories, bound generations together, and represented the history of a little community. In many ways, the worry about the windows was never just about the windows, but about so much more. Yes, those windows were precious and beautiful. But the fear of what would happen to those windows was also a fear about what would happen to the people of St. Peter's, and our future and legacy. If the windows couldn't speak of the congregation's faith, what would?

That summer, we worked with our insurance company to get the stained-glass repaired, getting estimates from companies capable of fixing the window with a hole. We also received estimates on the cost of removing those windows, storing them, and installing new ones. It took a while to repair, so as we worried and wondered, the hole in the crucifixion window remained. I'd stand in the pulpit and preach, looking at that cracked window, an open wound visible to all of us. It reflected our own broken hearts, right there next to our Savior on the cross.

During the time of the cracked window, my mom reminded me of the Japanese art of *kintsugi*. For centuries, artists in Japan have found ways to make beauty out of cracks. When a ceramic vase or cup is broken, an artist rejoins the pieces with a special lacquer made from tree sap mixed with gold or silver. When it is fired, the cracks become unique, almost jewelry-like seams. Instead of hiding the broken places, the artist highlights them, finding beauty in the imperfection.

I tried to shift my perception. Yes, the crack was an eyesore. But inspired by centuries of *kintsugi* artists, I started to see all the cracks as places where God could bring new beauty and hope into our faith-filled, imperfect vessels. Sometimes, we find the greatest hope in the hardest experiences and meaning on the other side of suffering. Like the gold tendrils in a piece of pottery, so often we discover Jesus and the depth of his love for us in the Golgothas of our lives, in the grief, loss, and brokenness.

In the late summer, a few months after our vote to close, the window restoration people arrived, demonstrating their trade with exceptional artistry and engineering skill. If only I could've fixed the holes in people's hearts with similar efficiency. But we can't fix grief. I couldn't undo the hurt. I couldn't make it any easier. Moving the windows wouldn't make it easier, either. This would be a temporary, expensive, and likely impossible fix. It wouldn't take away the pain. It might even make it harder. Clinging to what was so often makes it difficult to claim the new future given to us.

To move our focus beyond the windows, we needed to channel our energies into some productive planning. We had the opportunity to create our own legacy plan for how we wanted to share our financial resources after we closed. Like an estate plan put together before someone dies, we could dream together, as a congregation, about how to designate proceeds from the sale of our building and monies remaining in our endowment.

It would be one last, beautiful act of generosity from this congregation. In the years since, I've seen how people, like congregations, can be more generous in their death than they ever were in their life. People who live on fixed incomes as they age, the ones who penny-pinch for groceries and drive old cars, often have money set aside in life insurance policies or in the value of their homes. They craft their estates to allow for significant donations to congregations, seminaries, and organizations that matter to them. In sometimes surprising ways, they're generous in death in ways they couldn't have dreamed of while alive. It's beautiful to witness the joy and meaning that such anticipatory planning brings to the generous of heart.

The people of St. Peter's got excited about the possibilities of legacy generosity. As we engaged in conversation, I kept thinking about the many stories Jesus told about small things that became big. The little bit of yeast a woman stirred into her enormous bowl of flour became loaves and loaves of bread. The tiny mustard seed grew into a huge shrub where birds made a happy home. This is what happens when God's great dream of life and love for the world is realized—tiny things expand, grow, and spread. St. Peter's would become known for its enormous generosity through these legacy directives.

It's like when Jesus said, "unless a grain of wheat falls into the earth and dies, it remains just a single grain, but if it dies it bears much fruit" (John 12:24). Jesus said this just before his death. He tried to get his followers to understand that his death is not the end, but his promise of abundance and life can only come from his fully giving ourselves away. If we cling too much to this life, we'll lose all that we have. But if we let go, in trust, self-giving, and eventually in our dying, we will find abundant life. Or, as Eugene Petersen's Message translation says: "Listen carefully: Unless a grain of wheat is buried in the ground, dead to the world, it is never any more than a grain of wheat. But if it is buried, it sprouts and reproduces itself many times over. In the same way, anyone who holds on to life just as it is destroys that life. But if you let it go, reckless in your love, you'll have it forever, real and eternal." (John 12:24–25)[1]

None of us had harvested wheat before, but the people of St. Peter's caught on to this agrarian promise. They refused to keep those precious grains tucked in their pockets of grief or locked away in a glass case of nostalgia. Instead, they trusted that planting what little they had within the good soil of new partners and organizations in the wider church would keep their legacy alive in ever-expanding ways. They chose to be reckless in their love, trusting that God would bring big, reckless goodness through them.

The congregation met together one Sunday afternoon for a Legacy Workshop, led by Pastor Wagner, from the bishop's office. The workshop was essentially an exercise in writing our congregational will or estate plan. The workshop opened not with numbers and budgets but with stories about the ministry of St. Peter's over the decades. Pastor Wagner asked questions about key moments of mission and faithfulness. Energy from profound stories filled the room with enthusiasm and pride.

Pastor Wagner was masterful in guiding us on where to best plant those grain seeds. Many St. Peter's members came equipped with their idea of a top priority, some organization they wanted to be included in our legacy plans. We all had some pet project (quite literally, one person wanted us to give to the local animal shelter, which, though a worthy cause, was not connected with our mission or history). We brainstormed a long

1 Peterson, *The Message*, 1945.

list of deserving organizations. Ultimately, we narrowed the list to those causes that most closely aligned with St. Peter's commitments, values, and priorities.

Five percent of the net proceeds of the sale of the building would go to the World Hunger Appeal of our national denomination. Another five percent would go to Educación Popular en Salud, the organization in Chile that had been supported by St. Peter's for over a decade. We committed to reinvest the redevelopment grant money we received from the national church in two mission projects in New Jersey—one among Indian immigrants in central Jersey and another in the waterfront of Jersey City. Another significant gift would be given to the FISH Hospitality, the organization we partnered with to provide safe shelter for people without homes. A smaller gift was designated for the North Plainfield Rescue Squad. I was starting to imagine golden waves of grain rising up in fields, all because of our congregation's resolve to make a difference beyond ourselves.

The remaining assets would be given to the New Jersey Synod. To honor our organist, choir, and the many musicians who had served St. Peter's over the years, some money would be set aside to establish a scholarship for the education and training of church musicians. The remainder would be invested in the synod's Fund for Mission, to support congregations embarking on projects that serve their neighbors and share the gospel. And finally, some of the money would be given to St. Stephen's Lutheran Church, our receiving congregation.

To honor the leadership of the many pastors who had either served or been raised at St. Peter's over the decades, the most considerable portion of the building's sale was allocated to a seminary for the creation of a new scholarship fund. Our people were thrilled to make a tangible impact in shaping the future leaders of tomorrow.

Unfortunately, our unified commitment to support the training of pastors quickly turned divisive. The debate came as we decided *which* seminary would receive this significant gift. At the time, most Lutherans of our denomination in New England and the mid-Atlantic had connections to one of two seminaries in Pennsylvania, one in Philadelphia and the other in Gettysburg. Both seminaries seemed to be a good option. Both formed leaders to be sent out to serve the church. However, we could only choose to give the scholarship to one of them.

Struggling with this decision was among the more painful events of those last months. The arguments opened old wounds. I have seen similar disputes happen in families, where the decisions outlined in an estate plan led to conflict. Seldom is this just about greed; it usually points to deeper stories, old conflicts, or unaddressed issues.

So, it was for our people. Some members of the congregation felt that we should establish the scholarship at the Philadelphia seminary. Not only was it the closest geographically to us, but it was the seminary where St. Peter's members had gone for their training. Some of the pastors who served the church, including my predecessor, attended school here. However, others leaned toward setting up the scholarship at Gettysburg. This seminary had connections to a few of our people. However, the unspoken reason a few leaders supported the idea of giving the gift to Gettysburg was that it was *not* Philadelphia, where previous pastors had attended. I'll never know the extent of the conflict that preceded me, but that afternoon, I saw the resentments and pain that remained.

As this unfolded that afternoon, I felt such sadness. I had hoped we had worked through the conflict that had been a big part of the congregation before I arrived. While the whole story is complex and far more than I could understand, I did know that sides had been drawn, distrust had festered, and people had been deeply hurt. I shouldn't have been surprised that in this high-stakes moment, old animosity would surface. Often, in families and congregations, old hurts resurface in highly anxious moments and times of significant transition.

Most of the people present that day didn't have a preference. They trusted that either seminary would faithfully steward the gift. They simply wanted it to be used to support the formation of a future pastor, so that the whole church would benefit. After a close vote, the decision was finally made to give the gift to the seminary in Gettysburg. The seminary would use the gift well; pastors would receive a faithful formation and not have the burden of debt as they began their ministry. While it might seem a small decision, the depth of hurt caused by reaching it created cracks, fracturing our little community.

But as the Japanese potters remind us, the cracks are the exact places where we can find beauty. No vase, no stained-glass window, no community is perfect. We aren't expected to be. The real loveliness comes in the broken places.

As we worshipped that fall, the hole in the cross window was repaired. The cracks were hardly perceptible, but I could still see the tendrils of them in the wood of the cross. I wished I had some tree sap and gold dust to follow the way of *kintsugi,* making material the truth I knew of God's power to make beauty and goodness out of brokenness. This is the truth of the crucifixion, Christ brings life to dead places, forgiveness to cruel ones, healing to wounded ones. Our community, like the window, was still a bit cracked, still a bit hurt, still a bit angry, still a lot grieving. And yet, somehow, God would keep working through even us, like loaves of bread, a mustard shrub, or grains of wheat. Instead of hiding those cracks, the resilient beauty of God's love would become found in them, even in conflict, even in hurt, even in dying.

17

All Saints' Day 2009

Peter, the Rock

Then Jesus, again greatly disturbed, came to the tomb. It was a cave, and a stone was lying against it. Jesus said, "Take away the stone" (John 11:39).

By late fall, the various committees of St. Peter's completed their work. We packed the important papers, photos, and books in banker boxes to give to the archive center in Philadelphia. Homes were found for useful and holy things. Most of our households had settled on a plan for what would come next spiritually for them. The leaders proved themselves to be faithful stewards of the various objects and belongings of the church. Our legacy planning, even with its challenges, was finalized. Only one problem remained to be solved.

The building. Despite being on the market for months, we still hadn't found a buyer. The timing for the closure of our congregation couldn't have been worse. All our plans were coming to a head in the fall of 2009, a time of massive economic challenge. The recession meant most people and faith communities had limited, if any, resources to take on a big mortgage or buy a building. We worked with the congregations that rented our space for worship, but none had the funds to purchase our building. In the end, we decided to hand over the responsibility of selling the building to our partners in the synod office. Roy, George, and a few others volunteered to care for the building until we could hand it over to new owners. While letting go of control of this proved hard for some of our people, I felt a tremendous sense of relief and enormous gratitude for the willingness of our synodical staff to carry the weight of this.

All we had left to do was say goodbye. We set our final day of worship for All Saints' Sunday, chosen not just because of the timing, but also for its liturgical significance. The feast day reminded us that God weaves us into a great communion of saints, the church, here on earth and in heaven. St. Peter's lived as one tiny branch on this great big tree of God's people, and even though the one branch dies, the tree remains, flourishing. Most importantly, All Saints' Day grounds us in the promise of resurrection. Death is not the end. Life comes on the other side.

We planned two last worship services that day. One service would take place in the morning for the members of St. Peter's, and another would take place in the afternoon, when friends, neighbors, and partners would join us. The day began with our little community intimately gathered, people who had been through so much together, who had battled and praised, who had shown up and refused to give up on each other.

While some members of our community had moved and new ones had joined, the congregation remained essentially unchanged over the years. Many came to the corner of Mercer and Grove streets every Sunday for decades. Some had done so for the entirety of their lives. Sure, the pastor might be different, and various people would assist in leadership. Worshippers came and went, a new hymn might be introduced, and hopefully, some new ways of thinking would emerge in the sermons. But they knew when they walked into the bright red doors that someone would know their name and ask about their family. Someone knew if they liked sugar in their coffee. They remembered your favorite hymn. Many had a job to do. Most of them had a place where they'd always sit. They were known. And they knew others. They belonged.

At its best, belonging to a church community is different than joining a country club or a gym. It's not just an affiliation with people who are just like you or share the same hobbies, political party, or income bracket. Quite the opposite, Christian community pulls us into kinship with people whom we might never choose to have over for dinner. Congregations hold a common purpose of living out shared values and mutual commitments, building bonds of mutual care and trust in the process. Ideally, congregations become places where people are known, where their presence matters, and their absence is noticed. For the people of St. Peter's, they had spent decades creating a community of known-ness. This was a loss more substantial than any monetary, material, or measurable loss might be.

On that All Saints' morning, we were saying goodbye not only to a building and to long-present friends but also to this community of belonging. As we prepared for the morning's worship service, I was determined to be intentional about this goodbye. I wanted to give every member something tangible to take with them. They needed a material item that would not only help them remember the imperfect goodness of our congregation but would bless them as they stepped into a new future.

Throughout my life, my mom has taken moments of transition seriously. She marks them with meals, cakes, and gifts. Whether it's birthdays or anniversaries, graduations, or first days of school, Mom finds a way to make it momentous. On significant days, we ate pancakes from a red "You are Special Today" plate. She asked questions and created space to honor the moment. Most importantly, no change in life, including my first period, could happen without a homemade cake with buttercream frosting.

As my brother and I got older and we left home for one adventure or another, Mom prepared a special farewell dinner to bless us. Before going to college, starting a new job, studying abroad, or even taking a long road trip, Mom made us our favorite meal. After dessert, she would pull out a beautifully wrapped gift. These gifts weren't fancy. They were often simple and small enough to carry. It was her way of blessing us for our journeys.

When I left to live in Russia for a year, Mom gave me a coffee mug while keeping a matching one for herself. She explained how we would stay connected even if we were in opposite corners of the world, almost like sharing a cup of coffee in person. A silver angel traveled with me to study abroad in South Africa. I have little trinkets that I've zipped into backpacks and tucked into my purse, little tangible reminders that I was a cherished daughter. Those little gifts were not just a reminder of my mom's love for me; they pointed to the promise that is literally in the word "goodbye." The root of that word is "God be with you." Every time we say this, we name God's blessing. We tell another person that they carry God's love with them to the ends of the earth.

Inspired by my mom's blessing trinkets and intentional marking of transitions. I wanted to find a way to bless our community and say goodbye (God be with you) in a tangible way. I considered what special gift I could give to each person as we entered a new beginning. I needed to speak a blessing to them that would show how they carried Christ's power, presence, and goodness everywhere they went. Like those blessing gifts from my Mom, I wanted to do more than say those words, but give them something to hold onto and carry.

One of the newer stained-glass windows at St. Peter's depicts our patron, Simon Peter. He, like Elijah and David, stands in profile. Wearing a green robe with a crimson cape, Peter holds a set of keys in his hands as he looks up to the sky. Above him floats a banner with the words, "You are the Christ, the Son of the Living God." After Peter had said those words of bold faith and understanding, Jesus replied, "I tell you, you are Peter, and on this rock, I will build my church, and the gates of Hades will not prevail against it." (Matt. 16:18).

Inspired by Peter, whose name comes from the Greek word *petros,* which means rock, I gave each member of St. Peter's a rock. Not at all fancy, just a stone, worn smooth and polished. As I began my sermon that morning, I passed around baskets full of rocks, asking each of our members to choose one they wanted to keep. Over the decades, many saints of St. Peter's had been "rocks" for us, through their friendship and witness. Their presence in our lives provided a foundation. We leaned on them, were carried by them, and were "living stones" in our structures of faith. The little rocks we carried would remind us of the many people whose lives and faith built our community, whose faces, phrases, generosity, and kindnesses raced through their heads as we thought of saying goodbye. I expressed my gratitude for the ways they had been rocks for me.

That Sunday, the designated gospel reading told the story of Lazarus. It begins with Jesus meeting his friends Mary and Martha after their brother has died. They sealed their brother in the tomb with a big rock a few days earlier, naming the power and finality of death. In the shadow of death's power, the sisters turn to Jesus with grief and anger. Jesus weeps, too, his whole being wracked in sadness. Jesus joins in their suffering and feels it deeply with them.

But the story doesn't end with weeping. Instead, Jesus goes to the tomb and says, "Take away the stone." Jesus calls Lazarus out from that tomb. He restores him to life, removing the stone of death that once kept them separated. But this stone-moving, death-defying action didn't only happen that one time. On Easter morning, God, with the force of life that created the world, rolled away the stone that kept Jesus entombed. The gravestone could not contain Jesus and the power of his love buried inside the grave.

That All Saints' Day, as we said goodbye to our community of belonging and praise, I blessed them with rocks. In my sermon that morning, my voice catching in my throat with sadness, with trust, with blessing, I said, "These little rocks will, I pray, remind you of how grateful I have been for you. Carry these rocks which remind you that you are loved, by me, and more importantly, by our God known to us in Jesus Christ, who weeps with us, and takes away all the stones that keep us from abundant life."

18

All Saints' Day 2006

Petered Out

Jesus said, "You are the light of the world. A city built on a hill cannot be hid. People do not light a lamp and put it under the bushel basket; rather, they put it on the lampstand, and it gives light to all in the house. In the same way, let your light shine before others, so that they may see your good works and give glory to your Father in heaven" (Matthew 5:14–16).

After her brother's unexpected death, soccer legend and writer Abby Wambach spoke about the power of ritual and why funerals matter. Not a church person, and for good reason, having experienced the cruelty, judgment, and exclusion of religious people because of who she loves, Abby nonetheless reflected on the funeral held in the Roman Catholic church of her hometown. She talked about how a church sanctuary was the only place big enough to hold the depth of sadness and grief of that day. "I remember sitting in that church thinking, 'This is good. This is a good thing that they do,' because it's this ritual that gives you this container for all of the people and all of our energy and all of our sadness to be in the same place, to mourn this person that we loved."[1]

1. Wambach, *We Can do Hard Things*, 28:43.

Abby Wambach noted that the rituals surrounding death provide a needed container within which we can carry the weight of our mourning. Grief is heavy and cumbersome, impossibly messy and unwieldy. We need a container, some way to hold all our sorrows and worries, our hopes and fears altogether. Liturgy, the patterns of worship, old and time-tested, provide us with this container. We receive words to speak when we cannot think of them, songs to sing when we need to embody our sorrows and faith, and a community to hold us along the way. Liturgical worship creates a big enough vessel for all that we awkwardly hold.

Bearing grief is like moving a king-sized mattress. It lacks good handholds and doesn't fit through every door. The best way to carry it is in the company of others and with the help of some device to ease the load. Grief, too, requires other people. Our prayers, songs, and scripture become their own handles.

The people of St. Peter's broke for lunch after our morning worship. We reconvened a couple of hours later to prepare for the afternoon's service of Holy Closure. Over the decades, the congregation hosted many worship services outside of Sunday mornings. We welcomed our ecumenical partners in North Plainfield for holidays, civic times of mourning or celebration, and assorted funerals and weddings. We hosted meals, variety shows, fundraisers, and more. Over the years, the community had become adept at throwing parties, but this was our last hurrah, and everyone came together to make it happen.

The ushers greeted our guests, neighbors, and former members, as well as folks from St. Stephen's, our receiving congregation, and other Lutheran pastors and leaders. We set up extra chairs in the side wing of the sanctuary, a space that is usually empty, where worshippers sat under the watchful eyes of the colored stained-glass Peter, Elijah, and David, ever in profile. Earlier in the week, our weak little copy machine printed dozens of extra worship bulletins. Gloria and the rest of the Altar Guild pressed the paraments and polished the communion ware.

Leaders in our denomination had created the liturgy for that day. Someone pulled together the prayers and rituals that would accompany our community and those important to us through this ending. The words honored the past with gratitude and claimed the powerful truth of resurrection hope. In many ways, the service echoed the movements of a funeral service. There would be no burial, but we commended ourselves to God's care, and to a future we did not yet know. Just as Brian had taught me when

Charlie died, we did those three things we do at funerals: we remembered the congregation that died, remembered with care and consolation the ones who loved it, and mostly, we remembered the promises of God.

Right at 3:00 on All Saints' Day, Anders rang the bell, calling us to worship. A Norwegian in his eighties, Anders had grown up in Brooklyn and worked as a cook on a tugboat in the waterways around New York City. Anders married Hilda decades earlier, and he took pride in the fact that, unlike many men in his generation, he made the meals for his household. They were two immigrants who knew how to work hard, laugh often, and take their faith more seriously than they took themselves. Anders was crusty and tender, whose off-color jokes were outweighed by his commitment to St. Peter's. Often, we found Anders in the church kitchen preparing coffee and meals, washing dishes as he told stories and terrible puns.

As the bell rang to open worship, I prayed that someday that bell would ring again, calling a new community to worship in that building. But for now, it rang for us who had found grace and hope, community and courage, challenge and conflict in this sanctuary. One last time, we were called to the font and table, prayer and the Word, seeking souls finding belonging and our Savior in that beautiful place.

The organ music shook me from my reverie as we started to sing "For All the Saints." I felt the deepest affection for that old electric organ, played so capably by Julie, and the voices that filled the sanctuary. My song got stuck in my throat, and I remembered our friend Tom's words, "Let the community sing for you."

I stepped into the sanctuary and felt the strength of the voices and faith that echoed around me. "Thou wast their rock, their fortress and their might; thou, Lord, their captain in the well-fought fight."[2] The pews were full. I looked to the faces of St. Peter's members and friends, people who had been blessed by the faithful witness of this congregation, and others who were there to grieve and to support those who grieved.

The Bishop began by saying:

> We are here to celebrate the life of St. Peter's Lutheran Church, to give thanks to God for the gifts that have come to us and to others through this ministry, to acknowledge our sadness at the close of this ministry, and to affirm again our faith in Jesus Christ. Let us be grateful for God's gifts, honest about our sorrow, open in love, trusting in Jesus Christ, the only head of the church. The service

2. Evangelical Lutheran Church in America, *Evangelical Lutheran Worship*, 422.

> today marks a passage for this congregation. A ministry is coming to a close; something new is about to be born. God is calling the members of this congregation to a new ministry. Congregations are formed and congregations are disbanded, but the Lord our God reigns forever.[3]

Then Grace stood up to tell the history of St. Peter's. EPES, our housing ministry, and the numerous organizations the congregation had supported over the years were highlights in the narrative of the congregation's generosity. Grace named the people who had blessed her life, including the pastors who served faithfully and the parishioners who had entered the ministry. Grace had lived for 80 of Peter's 117 years, her own story woven through it all.

Pastor Wagner followed Grace's own eulogy with these words

> How can we thank you, O God, for the ministry of this congregation over these past 117 years?
> For every person who has shown the love of Christ to another,
> for every quiet act of service which helped another,
> for every song of praise offered to you from the depths of a grateful heart,
> for every prayer uttered here, which you gave honor and glory,
> for all the ways in which you have guided and directed your people
> for all these gifts of ministry.
> For these things, we give you thanks.[4]

Clara, the nurse and Bible teacher, read the readings appointed for All Saints' Sunday. She spoke of God swallowing up death forever and wiping tears from faces, mourning and crying and pain becoming non-existent. Then, I stepped up the few steps into the box of the high German pulpit, standing where I had learned to preach. I looked out at that congregation assembled and into the eyes of people who had grown to trust my words, even as I learned to trust them myself.

I read, for the second time that day, the gospel for All Saints' Day, where John tells of Jesus weeping and Lazarus stumbling from the tomb, bound up in burial clothes. I stood in the pulpit, praying that the Spirit would give me the strength to speak words of hope to our people, neighbors, and friends. I began by sharing a conversation I had with Grace over the summer. We had been conversing about everything the congregation

3. New Jersey Synod, *Celebration of Ministry*. 2.

4. New Jersey Synod, *Celebration of Ministry*, 3.

had done over the years and how we could no longer do it. She said, a bit tongue-in-cheek, "Well, I guess we just sort of petered out."

I shared how that phrase generally means fading away, like a flame in an oil lamp that starts to flicker but diminishes as the oil runs out. One of the etymological explanations of that phrase connects it back to St. Peter himself, who, as a disciple, is sometimes described as "petering out" in following Jesus. He fell asleep in the garden, denied Jesus around the fire, and ran away when it got tough.

But that doesn't tell our story, I told the congregation filling our small sanctuary. The closing of St. Peter's was the opposite of denial or failure. It was an act of faithfulness.

Peter's story has more to it than just denial, too. After meeting the resurrected Christ, the Spirit filled him with power, and Peter went on to preach and bring thousands to Christ. The light of Christ that radiated from Peter did not "peter out." The chosen leader among Jesus' followers did not fade or fizzle away but grew brighter and bolder.

I stood in the pulpit a few steps up from the sanctuary floor that afternoon. I looked into the eyes of the people I had grown to love and told them that they had redefined this phrase "petering out." Their ending was not a dimming of their light. Their radiant faith would not flicker into oblivion. Instead, by their faithful courage, they were letting their light so shine, even as the winds of change buffeted and tears flowed.

From that high pulpit, for the last time, I preached. While our congregation lived this, I told our friends and neighbors about St. Peter's unique Christmas Eve tradition. Like many congregations, we sang "Silent Night" by candlelight at the end of the service. We lit the candles from the bright flame of the Christ Candle, which symbolizes the light of Christ that cannot be extinguished. Not by tears, not by endings, not by death. Each person carries that light. This, of course, is not unique. What was distinctive about Christmas Eve at St. Peter's was that at the end of worship, the congregation didn't blow out their candles; instead, they carried those lit candles down the aisle and out of the sanctuary.

No, we were not petering out. The light still shined. Brighter than ever. Now we would carry that light to the places God would lead us.

Somehow, I made it through those words without my voice cracking, although I did shed tears while serving communion, holding the silver plate given in memory of Charlie, placing bits of bread in familiar hands. After communion, we relinquished the historical records and our legacy directives to the Bishop. The congregation membership lists were entrusted to the people of St. Stephen's and their pastor, my husband, Clark, who would receive our people into their care. Then the Bishop said, "I declare the congregation to be closed in the name of the Father, and of the Son, and of the Holy Spirit. May the witness of its people continue undiminished and empowered by Jesus Christ, the Lord of the Church. Amen."[5]

As they did at the end of worship every spring before taking a break for the summer, our choir sang a blessing, the well-known Lutkin Benediction. But this time, their voices were bolstered by the choir at St. Stephen's and the alumni of our choir. In four-part harmony, words first spoken by Moses to Aaron and the Israelites echoed in the sanctuary. Among the oldest words of scripture, these words that have endured centuries, persecutions, countless farewells, and more. "The Lord bless you and keep you. The Lord lift His countenance upon you and give you peace. The Lord make His face to shine upon you and be gracious unto you."[6]

Then Anders went to the bell tower and rang the bell. Slow and steady, long, deep toll after another, the bell rang one hundred and seventeen times. One toll for every year of ministry. We all sat quietly as the echoes of the bell rang around us. It seemed like an eternity, those tones reverberating in our bodies, one hundred and seventeen tolls.

In my mom's hometown of Bruning, Nebraska (population 281), the church bell rang whenever a person died. My mom remembers stopping in the playground as a kid and counting the bells as they rang, knowing that the number of rings reflected the age of whoever had died. People in their little town stopped to listen, to acknowledge the reality of loss, of death, of the grief that now accompanied someone, many someones. When the bell tolled, the world stopped.

The world seemed to stop the day St. Peter's bell tolled for a final time. Perhaps others in the neighborhood stood still, too, as the bell rang again and again and again. They might not have known the heartbreak that was unfolding down the road from them, or the sadness that weighed so heavily on a bunch of Lutherans and their friends. I hope they perceived a measure of hope in that bell that rang, persistent hope, the stubborn kind that refuses to give up.

5. New Jersey Synod, *Celebration of Ministry*, 6.

6. Lutkin, *The Lord Bless You.*

Listening to the repeated echoes of the bell that day, I thought about the John Donne poem that asks us, "For whom does the bell toll?" The poem begins:

> No man is an island,
> Entire of itself.
> Each is a piece of the continent,
> A part of the main.
> If a clod be washed away by the sea,
> Europe is the less.[7]

The borough of North Plainfield, that neighborhood, our Church, this world, is the less because of St. Peter's ending. The full sanctuary that afternoon demonstrated how our small church had a profound impact on the lives of many. Just as even a clod of dirt left a whole continent a bit less, so too is the world, our church, less because our little church in North Plainfield died. Still, it is heartbreaking to write it. Our little church died.

Our little church died.

John Donne ends "No Man Is an Island" with the line, "Ask not for whom the bell tolls; it tolls for thee."[8] We're all bound together, in our losses and lives, in our dying and rising. It was this hope that I clung to as the bell tolled at 4:30 that afternoon. Our congregation was not an island unto itself, nor were we the entirety of the Christian church. We were a beautiful part of it, a vital, unique, and precious part of it, but we were not the continent. We mattered, as with a little clod washed away by the sea. But the continent didn't sink. God's church would continue, and so would our people. The bell tolled 117 times for us . . . and for the God we loved.

7. Donne, *No Man is an Island.*

8. Donne, *No Man is an Island.*

19

November 2009

Jesus on the Cross

I want to know Christ and the power of his resurrection and the sharing of his sufferings by becoming like him in his death, if somehow, I may attain the resurrection from the dead (Philippians 3:10–11).

EVEN THOUGH WE HAD officially ended our ministry, we were not yet done at St. Peter's. In the days that followed our last service, the building buzzed with activity as our people finished loading and cleaning. I stuck to my office, packing up my books and sorting through papers. All those tasks distracted us, helping to diminish the raw power of our grief.

But grief is a sneaky beast and makes itself known. Most people define grief too narrowly. We permit people to grieve for close loved ones who have died. But grief comes whenever there is loss. Any loss. We grieve the end of a job, the death of a dog, when a friend moves away, or when our body stops working because of injury or age. Whenever we experience a loss, grief follows. Generally speaking, the more significant the loss, the more substantial the grief.

When a congregation closes for good, its members experience many losses. They lose a community and their Sunday morning destination. Without that familiar space offering weekly solace, support, and spiritual sustenance, it can feel like the door to God is closed. Or, as if the Lord has become unavailable. It's not only a felt loss in the present moment, but a sense of being severed from all the people, traditions, and stories of the past. A church's closure can also mean the loss of an imagined, hoped-for future.

Even more, for those most deeply involved in acts of service at St. Peter's, a large void of meaning and purpose was emerging. While activity and responsibility to our small church's ministry stretched many people thin, it also gave them a life-giving purpose. They were now about to lose this expression of themselves. They would have to find new ways to serve and do the work that not only benefited others but also brought them joy.

Far and away, though, for me and for everybody else, the biggest loss came in the dispersion of our people. Many of the friendships between our people would continue, especially for those who would move together to our receiving congregation. However, for many others, attending St. Stephen's didn't make sense. Some had connections elsewhere or had moved a distance away. They would find a congregation much closer to home.

Our staff was hit hard by layers of grief. Not only did we lose our primary source of income and meaningful work, but we also lost the relationships inherent in this line of work. Pam was so much more than just the church secretary. She'd become friends with the many people who came through our doors, who would stop at her desk. They had spent time sitting in one of the folding chairs by her desk to talk for a while, and were known by the pitch and timbre of their "hellos" on the phone. She would be saying final goodbyes to these dear friends.

Julie, our director of music, didn't just play the organ or lead our small choir. Lingering after rehearsals became her habit as she checked in on our people and listened to stories about their grandchildren. She hung out in the Fellowship Hall after worship for treats and conversation. Church work is not just work, and it's certainly more than a job. It's a calling. With this vocation comes the beautiful gift of people who burrow their way into our hearts.

As part of the congregation's legacy planning work, the staff received thoughtful severance pay. This was done with affection and genuine acknowledgement of our commitment, faithfulness, and hard work. St. Peter's last gift to us was this bridge of support as we found new positions and sorted through our grief.

It is the expectation within my denomination that when a pastor leaves a congregation, they intentionally shift their relationships with the people they serve. I've found it's inauthentic to sever all connections completely, but it's generally a wise idea for all clergy exiting their community to step away and truly leave. After All Saints' Day, I was no longer the pastor to the people of St. Peter's. They were now under the care of other clergy and spiritual leaders. If one of "my people" died, someone else would do the funeral. Another pastor would show up at their bedside if they were hospitalized. This was right and good. But it was hard. It meant I said a faster goodbye than I realized to a whole lot of people I had come to love.

In those days immediately following our last service, my time in the office felt off-kilter and heavy, out of our usual rhythm of preparing for the next Sunday's worship or an upcoming holiday. However, people continued to come to church. Keys would jingle as they opened the side door. Familiar footsteps echoed down the hallway. Some came to finish packing up the last of our treasures or deliver items to local churches. Others, it seemed, made up reasons to come in, to be in the building, to just be with each other. We collected everyone's keys. Well, almost everyone's keys. Roy, George, and a few others would tend to the building until it sold.

On my final day, I walked through the building one last time, stopping in the sanctuary to privately sort through my sadness and gratitude. I sat down on the carpeted steps near the altar and looked out over the empty space. I imagined our people sitting in the places where they'd always sit. I had come to know each one, the person and their place. I thanked God for them, for the ways they blessed me. I begged forgiveness for the ways I might have hurt them, trying to let go of the ways they had hurt me. God had entrusted them to me. For the briefest time, I had the privilege of being their pastor, but now it was time to let them go.

I stared at the stained-glass window of Jesus hanging on the cross, the cracks still visible. The crucifixion image in that window is hardly unique; similar depictions can be found in windows and paintings throughout the Western world. Ours was a peculiarly muscular Jesus with arms outstretched, wide enough to hold the whole world and the vastness of our collective grief. Nails pierced his hands and side, and a crown of thorns wrapped his head. The sky behind him is dark and stormy with bloated clouds ready to unleash a torrent of rain.

As I sat silently staring across that sanctuary, I felt this deep, compassionate care coming my way from the very Jesus I was gazing at. How strange that colored glass can convey empathy and divine presence. I thought of the last words Jesus spoke from the cross in the gospel of John: "It is finished."

This statement doesn't mean that Jesus' life is over. Instead, it reveals a powerful theological truth: on the cross, Jesus fulfilled the tasks for which he came to earth. The Greek root *teleo* is behind the word we see translated as "finished." *Telos* is that ultimate goal or purpose of a particular project or assignment. Jesus did what he needed to: he came to earth, drawing all people to himself, making us whole in the process. That's telos. Work completed.

The writer of John understood that Jesus' crucifixion was not a moment of failure, but of glory. The crucifixion was always bound up in the resurrection. Just days before his death, Jesus tells his friends, "The hour has come for the Son of Man to be glorified. Very truly, I tell you, unless a grain of wheat falls into the earth and dies, it remains just a single grain, but if it dies it bears much fruit." (John 12:23–24).

Those words had echoed in my heart since we reflected on them during our legacy workshop. As I sat on the red-carpeted steps of St. Peter's that day, I prayed that our people would come to know this glory. I trusted that God would bring us through this loss, that we would experience community again, joy in worship, and meaning in service. I prayed that somehow, the grain of St. Peter's planted into the soil would bear all kinds of fruit.

With the advantage of a rearview mirror, now, I see the brightness of glory found in the fruit from those grains once buried deep in the soil. But in the sorrow of my final week, it was barely a shimmer. I tried to trust that God would do again what God had done before. The people, the ones I imagined present with me in my prayer, had taught me this truth. Now we had to step forward, like Abraham and Sarah, to the place where God would lead us.

As I sat in the quiet of the sanctuary that day, I heard the big red doors opening on the other side of the building. Gloria and George had come to say goodbye and to collect my keys. I gave Jesus in the window a nod of gratitude, looked around the sanctuary one last time, and took a deep breath for courage to step into the unknown of what was to come for me personally. I went to my office (mine for only a few more moments), put on my coat, and felt a curious affection for the furnishings and décor that had made this a first home for my pastoral ministry.

As I walked out the side door, I turned to give Gloria and George each a hug full of gratitude. Then, as had become my habit, I turned around and grabbed the metal door handles inscribed with those fish. A little tug to make sure they were latched, and indeed they were. The doors were closed. The church was locked. It was finished. *Telos.*

20

Winter 2009–2010

Holy Saturday

Do not fear, for I have redeemed you;
I have called you by name; you are mine.
When you pass through the waters, I will be with you,
and through the rivers, they shall not overwhelm you;
When you walk through fire, you shall not be burned, and the flame
shall not consume you (Isaiah 43:2).

My dad was a voracious reader. He left books around the house, piled up at church, in his car. He read with a black pen in his hand, ready to underline a passage, write a question, or comment in the margins. He always kept a pen hooked over some of the pages, a bookmark of sorts to save his place and ensure he had a pen in hand when he picked up the book again. In his last months of life, as chemotherapy and the exhaustion of illness slowed his quick mind, he read less and more slowly. After Dad died, we found his black pen tucked in the middle of a book he never finished, *Between Cross and Resurrection: A Theology of Holy Saturday,* written by Scottish theologian Alan E. Lewis, who himself was dying of cancer.

Lewis wrote about that day between Good Friday and Easter Sunday. On that empty Saturday between Christ's death and the resurrection, nothing obvious happens. Jesus' friends observed the Sabbath with sorrow and heartbreak. It was a time of silence, of waiting, of tears. A sense of absence dominated that second day before the women found an empty tomb. Yesterday Jesus died, and tomorrow Jesus will rise. But that Saturday sat in between, where both seemingly contradictory realities are held together—despair and hope, grief and joy, death and life. Lewis writes:

> We have always said, however, that at the boundary, which is the second day, it is possible and necessary to look both ways, and that the boundary conjoins what it also divides. But how can these antitheses, these contradictory worlds at either side of their Saturday border, be united and held together in our faith, our understanding, and our ways of life and death? How is it possible for there to be a day in history which both the day after the end of life *and* the day before the end of death, the day which remembers Christ's failure and his Father's, *and* the day which hopes for his and for God's future and therefore for our own? By now, we have felt the anguished trauma in the cancer ward and the prognosis of no more pain and suffering in the future . . . If the gospel story is that *both* kinds of scenarios are serious and true, that it is in the very world of sickness and death and sin that joy and play take place, and Christ is Lord, then it is only in the context of injustice, negativity, and despair that we dare to speak of hope.[1]

The weeks after St. Peter's closed felt like Holy Saturday days for me and many in our congregation. Resurrection and new life do not come immediately. Space and silence happen first. We need time to feel the heartbreak, the anger, the grief, and the shame. Sometimes we get stuck in Good Friday, and other times we rush too quickly to Easter, but Holy Saturday provides a moment of time to be in that liminal space, caught between two realities of death and life.

After St. Peter's closed, thanks to the generous severance I received, I had some time to live in my Holy Saturday. I needed space and quiet for restoration. In those initial weeks after the closing, I felt unmoored, unsure of what to do with myself. This unanchored, drifting feeling reminded me of an experience I had a year earlier on a beach in India.

My brother and sister-in-law, who lived in southern India at the time, drew my husband, Clark, and me there. We spent a few days in Varkala, a quaint and quirky beach town in the eastern state of Kerala, on the Indian Ocean. The town sat up on a cliff, with cafés, shops, and hotels along a sidewalk that overlooked the water. Each day, we enjoyed a leisurely breakfast

1. Lewis, *Between Cross and Resurrection*, 66–67.

with a sea view and then walked down the long staircase to the beach. We sat under colorful umbrellas hammered into the sand. Men walked by with bags of coconuts to sell, ready to crack one open for any tourist's refreshment.

The water felt cool on the hot days. While not particularly deep, the ocean had a strong rip current. Whistles and admonishments echoed from the lifeguards, warning people who swam out too deep and too far to the dangerous side of the beach. One afternoon, as I floated and played in the water, I was unaware of the current pulling me far away from where I began. That is, until I heard the lifeguards yelling at me to move closer to shore. I tried to do what they said, since I could still touch the bottom. Still, the sand was moving beneath my feet, moving out to sea. Despite some quick attempts at swimming and even walking toward safety, the riptide pulled me farther and farther out.

I tried to stay calm, but no matter how hard I tried, I couldn't get closer to shore. Clark wasn't far from me and instantly saw the panic in my eyes. He held my hand and brought the steady presence I married him for. Soon, a stranger grabbed my other hand. A fit, dark-haired man with kind eyes spoke in an Italian accent, reminding me to stay calm. Slowly and steadily, they guided me safely to shore.

They settled me on our beach blanket, assuring me I was okay. The Italian man returned to his young children playing in the sand. I sat under a colorful umbrella, grateful for the warm, solid earth beneath me. Clark picked up his book but held my hand as he read. I stared at the waves, trying to slow down my heart and breathe normally again.

The water where I stood had been no more than four feet deep, and yet, I nearly drowned. Perhaps that's an exaggeration, but I didn't have the strength against the force of the current, which kept pulling my feet out from under me. The ground lost solidity. The shifting sand of the ocean floor kept dragging me with it. I could not save myself. Only because of the response of my partner and a perfect stranger did I manage to get out of the waves.

In the weeks after St. Peter's closed, I depended on many people to carry me through the uncertain time. The ground itself seemed unstable. Clark, as he displayed in the water of the Indian Ocean, was a steady presence for me. My mom listened. As Thanksgiving rolled around, a few weeks after our last worship service, Brent and Connie, back from India, and other old friends came to our house. We played games for four straight days, only stopping to prepare and eat good food. In the steadiness and presence of other people, I experienced God's promise: "When you pass through the waters, I will be with you, and through the waves, they shall not overwhelm you." (Isa. 43:2). I prayed that steadying forces would be present for the people of St. Peter's, too.

That first Christmas without parish duties was hard for me. It was hard for others, too. Debbie later told me that she and Ethan skipped church on Christmas Eve, unable to imagine being anywhere but our little brick church in North Plainfield. Holy days and special festivals are especially tough after a loss. They accentuate what is missing, spotlighting the person or community that should be there but isn't. Grace wouldn't be singing 'O Holy Night' this year. Friends wouldn't be sitting in their self-assigned seats in the pews. I didn't have a sermon to write or worship to plan. In many ways, others and I were trying to stay upright as the sea moved underfoot, the current tugging at our stability and confidence. But we did not drift away; others grabbed our hands, held us steady, invited us to worship, and kindly listened to our grief.

Sometime that winter, as I dug through boxes full of objects from St. Peter's, I found a calligraphy art print that had hung in the sacristy of St. Peter's. Gloria gave it to me as she packed up some last things in the building. It held the words of Martin Luther's sacristy prayer written in colorful medieval script:

> Lord God, you have appointed me as a pastor in your Church,
> but you see how unsuited I am to meet so great and difficult a task.
> If I had lacked your help, I would have ruined everything long ago.
> Therefore, I call upon you: I wish to devote my mouth and my heart to you;
> I shall teach the people. I myself will learn and ponder diligently upon your Word.
> Use me as your instrument—but do not forsake me,
> for if ever I should be on my own, I would easily ruin it all. Amen.[2]

I had thanked Gloria, put the calligraphy into a box, and promptly forgot about it. Later, when I discovered it again, I felt the weight of the accusation in the words. A profound sense of failure at the end of St. Peter's life overwhelmed me. I worried that I had, in Luther's words, "ruined it all." Would the description of my North Plainfield ministry always be that I let my people down and I disappointed my Bishop, colleagues, and perhaps

2. Luther, *Luther's Works, Vol.5, 123.*

the whole Church? That scared me. The guilt pulled at me like an undertow, the hefty weight of my failure ruining it all.

In the winter after St. Peter's closed, Clark and I found support and homemade pizza at the home of a former seminary professor and her husband, mentors who became friends. With the kind of courage that I came to know as their personal sturdiness of faith, they entered the tumultuous waters of my grief and listened to me share feelings of deep and raw shame. Like the Italian dad who had held my hand in the wave, and with their own knowledge of both me and of God, this couple led me back to solid ground. We ate warm homemade brownies that tasted like chocolate hope.

Our friends repeated back to me the very truths I had been telling my people in the pews: *Petering out* wasn't about failure, but courage; endings are natural, goodness will emerge on the other side; God will do a new thing in and through us because this is what God always has done. They helped me alter the way I told my own story. It didn't deserve to be a story of defeat, but rather one of faithful leading, even when the waters rose, and the waves threatened.

The stories that we tell matter. Like a vinyl record cursed with a scratch, I was stuck repeating the narrative that I had ruined it all. But these friends pointed me to other realities that I had ignored or couldn't see through the cloud of shame. This change in storytelling doesn't rewrite history or revise reality. St. Peter's still ended its ministry. Plenty of hearts were still broken, including my own. But the core theme of that church closure didn't have to be failure. The story had a more complex and ongoing plot, one that involved bold courage and persistent faith.

Over pizza and brownies on many Friday nights, these friends helped me to re-story my experience at St. Peter's. Reframing the stories we tell isn't just a practice within narrative psychotherapy and spiritual direction. It's how we intentionally interpret experiences in such a way as to make us experts of our own lives. Giving proper shape to the stories we tell about ourselves can lead to healing, liberation, and wholeness. Often this is called "re-authoring" or "re-storying" our lives.

In her book introducing narrative therapy, Alice Morgan, writes:

> As humans, we are interpreting beings. We all have daily experiences of events that we seek to make meaningful. The stories we have about our lives are created through linking certain events together in a particular sequence across a time period and finding a way of explaining or making sense of them. This meaning forms

> the plot of the story. We give meaning to our experiences constantly as we live our lives. A narrative is like a thread that weaves the events together, forming a story.[3]

In the first months after I locked the church door for a final time, I kept telling the story of my failure, replaying moments of my leadership deficiencies, and rehashing every mistake that came to mind. Like an editor of a reality TV show, I only pulled into the reel the parts of the story that portrayed me as incompetent, young, timid, and ineffective. All I saw were the frames showing our failures. But this was an incomplete, if not false, narrative.

So, with the help of wise and steady companions, I began to "re-story" my three years at St. Peter's. I vividly reclaimed stories of the faithfulness of our community. I privileged stories about our creativity as we fought to make a go of it. I remembered the many genuine comments about my strength as a leader and the care I delivered. I recalled the beautiful and healing conversations and experiences in our congregation throughout the final months. As I replayed in my head stories of our faithfulness, a "thick" reality came into play. "Thin" conclusions are shallow and often negative themes that disempower people, name problems, and highlight dysfunctions. They usually reflect cultural hierarchies and relationships of power. "Once thin conclusions take hold, it becomes easy for people to engage in gathering evidence to support these dominant problem-saturated stories."[4] Thickening our stories is about complicating the narrative, inviting in new perspectives, and remembering with rich, complex details.

Over time, like a snowball rolling down a hill, my story about St. Peter's accumulated strength and thickness. I learned to tell my story not as one where I "ruined it all" but where, by the power of the Spirit, we all gave it all for Jesus' sake, for the good and benefit of the whole church.

This process of "re-storying" the closing of St. Peter's didn't magically reopen the church. What it did was restore the truth of God's goodness, featuring the resolve of our community as we pursued God's guidance. In remembering a deeper, more complicated story, God put me back together again; I was re-membered. I no longer stood on the thin, moving ground of an incomplete and negative story, but on the firm foundation of the complicated, thick, and ultimately, faithful story.

3. Morgan, *What is Narrative Therapy?*, 5.
4. Morgan, *What is Narrative Therapy?*, 13.

As Christians, Jesus thickens the narratives of our lives even further. His story of life on the other side of death and salvation found in self-giving frames our own experiences. Christ's Easter resurrection is the ultimate "re-storying." Without it, Good Friday would have just been another day of executions and oppression, and Saturday would have been the first of more days of disappointment and despair ahead. We'd be stuck with thin stories that tell the lies of God's absence, of the empire's complete power, of the small being forgotten.

On that first Holy Saturday, we presume that Jesus' friends did nothing but sit together before the silence of death, which must've echoed as loudly as resounding thunder. But in their emptiness, the steadfastness of God's enduring presence remained. Even in their despair, they weren't alone. God was with them, even then. And they were with one another.

Could those friends of Jesus have spent that Saturday telling stories? They had more than enough thin stories to go around, ones of failure and despair. They knew of denials at dawn, sleepiness in the garden, and abandonment at Golgotha. But surely, they must have also remembered the stories of lost sheep being found, multiplied loaves creating banquets, Lazarus being raised, and seeds dying to become fruit. Maybe they even broke some bread and passed a cup. I'm pretty certain they spent time in quiet acts that re-membered them. On that day of emptiness, God formed them back into the people they knew themselves to be, even in their despair, even before they could comprehend what would come when the dawn of Easter came.

On a wintry day during my first jobless months after our church's closure, I received a call from one of my closest friends from seminary. After too many years of her vocation being stifled and hindered, Ann would finally be ordained. She needed these sacred and colorful accessories that pastors wear for worship, and commissioned me to make them for her. I designed a set of scarves and capes (stoles and chasubles) to be pieced from vibrant dupioni silk, with subtle patterns and images sewn into the pieced shades of colored fabric. The red set for Pentecost came alive with the shapes of flames and movement like the wind. The white stole and chasuble, worn at Easter, Christmas, and All Saints, included bits of gold with rays of light bursting from the center. The designs on the blue for Advent were a bit more subdued but included a nearly hidden Mary with a round belly and a bright morning star of light in dusk's dim, dark blue.

I cut apart this beautiful silk and carefully sewed it back together, piecing the fabric into a textile collage. Sometimes the voices and music of public radio kept me company. But most of the time, I worked in silence, lost in memory. Scenes from my time at St. Peter's played in my head—the conflicts and confrontations, the mistakes made. But also, the deep faithfulness, the courageous truth-telling, the sacrificial giving, the laughter and kindness, the delicious meals and beautiful music, the conversations, and the silence. While layering colors of fabric, sewing a complicated pattern for Annie's vestments, I built a thick story for myself, for our people, strong enough to withstand the waves, the undertow, the doubts, and the fears. I remembered, and in so doing was re-membered, put back together.

The sun rose on that first Easter morning. Dawn arrived. In an act of love to their assumed-dead friend, the women carried myrrh into the graveyard, only to find an empty tomb and be told of a risen Savior. That is the story we tell, and it's a story so trustworthy that I've bet my life on it. Holy Saturday wasn't the end of the early disciples' story, and it isn't the end of our story. The hope for new life I fiercely clung to in those months after our ending arose in ways I could never have imagined. For some at St. Peter's, this hope took years to discover. Others in the congregation are still looking. But God's resurrecting power for new life worked in and among all of us in powerful ways. Good Friday does not end the story, nor does Holy Saturday. The waves do not overtake us.

21

2010-Present

Legacy

For as the rain and the snow come down from heaven
and do not return there until they have watered the earth,
making it bring forth and sprout,
giving seed to the sower and bread to the eater
so shall my word be that goes out from my mouth.
it shall not return to me empty,
but it shall accomplish that which I purpose
and succeed in the thing for which I sent it
(Isaiah 55:10–13).

Orson Welles wrote, "If you want a happy ending, that depends, of course, on where you stop the story."[1] If I were to stop in the winter of 2009, the story of St. Peter's would be one of devastating grief and failure. But the same would be true if we stopped reading the story of the Israelites as they wandered through the desert, still not yet in the promised land. The same is true, too, if we were to end the story of Jesus when they placed him in the tomb, the stone rolled as a period at the end of his life's sentence. The same would happen if we stopped Paul's story when he was known as Saul, the

1. Welles, *Big Brass Ring.*

persecutor of Christians. But those stories continued to tell of unexpected new identities, freedom, and life.

Clark and I moved to Iowa a little over a year after St. Peter's closed. A congregation in Davenport, on the banks of the Mississippi River, invited me to serve as one of their associate pastors. At a conference with church leaders serving throughout Iowa, one of my new colleagues exclaimed, "So, you're from the East Coast?!" I nodded, surprised that he knew we had relocated from New Jersey. Then he laughed, "I meant the east coast of Iowa, along the Mississippi." The big river might not be the Atlantic Ocean that borders the Jersey shore, but it shapes much of the economy, history, geography, and culture of the "east coast" of Iowa.

Over the next few years, we settled into life in Iowa and brought two curious and creative kids into the world. When they were small, we took a day trip to an environmental education center north of us, near the Maquoketa River, which flows into the Mississippi. We wandered through displays showing the root depths of native prairie grasses alongside taxidermized ducks and rodents set up in dioramas. Our kids watched native frogs and freshwater fish as they paddled around in aquariums.

One wall held a map of the Mississippi River basin, the enormous continental funnel of rivers, streams, and creeks that drain into the Mississippi as it widens before spilling out into the Gulf of Mexico. I hadn't realized the breadth of the Mississippi watershed until that moment. Most of the land and water between the Rocky Mountains and the Appalachian Mountains feed into this big river close to our home. From every direction, the water flows down and out with gravity, all converging toward the geographic center of the continent.

I stared at the map, which urged visitors at the environmental center to take the stewardship of our water seriously, given how interconnected we are with it. But I couldn't help but think about God's work in the world. In the words of the prophet Isaiah, God's words rain down from the sky and cascade into our lives, accomplishing the purpose for which God sent them. We're carried in that current until, like water that evaporates into the clouds, we return to God to join with all the saints. Together, we all flow toward God's loving, generous, deep, and wide mercy.

Water has a way of moving with gravity toward the lowest place. This resembles the way of Jesus, who emptied himself and became human, touching lepers and washing feet. As his followers, we aim to live with intentional downward mobility, serving and sharing, and pouring cups of water for the least of these. The resources God entrusts to us were never meant to be dammed up, stuck up in some reservoir where only a few can enjoy them, or saved in containers for some feared future. Instead, it's all meant to be shared, given away, flowing away from us.

While we waited for the building to sell, St. Peter's legacy gifts, our hopes, and our prayers for generosity were held back by a dam. (This is a metaphor, of course. Though I'd be willing to bet that others said this word and other choice words over the long, frustrating months when the building sat empty on the market.) But then, one day in December of 2011, my phone rang from an unknown Chicago number. I heard a voice say, "Hi, Sara. I'm the director of ELCA World Hunger. I want to thank you and the people of St. Peter's for this most extraordinary gift." I don't remember the details of the conversation. I only remember being immediately aware that the day we prayed for had finally arrived. St. Peter's church building was sold, and with that sale, the legacy funds, at long last, had been distributed.

I contacted my colleagues in the synod office in New Jersey, and they confirmed the news. The building had indeed been sold, and the gifts dispersed. The waters began to flow figuratively and literally. The leaders at the New Jersey Synod began to share the proceeds from the sale as soon as they could, following the legacy wishes that St. Peter's had laid out years earlier.

WORLD HUNGER

The first call I received came from the director of our denomination's World Hunger program. Over $30,000 from the sale of our building sales to people with great need around the world. For decades, the people of St. Peter's budgeted and sacrificed to give a fraction of that for the sake of hungry people. To be able to give so much away felt like a miracle of loaves and fishes enormity.

After they received our gift in 2012, the leaders at ELCA World Hunger immediately put that money to use in the projects they were launching. Through our partners in the global Lutheran Church, the ELCA World Hunger Teams have developed relationships with on-the-ground organizations in every corner of the world. At the time, they funded work happening in various corners of the world, from India to Milwaukee to Zimbabwe. They included support for the Evangelical Lutheran Development Service (ELDS) in Malawi, which works to bring about sustainable agricultural changes in rural Malawi. They invested in goats and pigs, a community seed bank, and other agricultural projects.

One creative project in Malawi developed a savings and loan opportunity providing microloans to women to invest in small businesses or to buy seeds and fertilizer for their subsistence farms. One of the participants, Fyness Phiri, was one of the poorest people in her village. She relied on her neighbors for money to purchase food for herself and her four children. However, with the community support and financial investment from this project, Fyness soon could produce enough food to feed her family, pay back her loan, and even sell extra food at the market.

"Since I joined the project," Fyness said, "my life has completely changed. I have food in my house, and I'm able to send my children to school. Because of the knowledge [I've gained], I will be able to continue and help others even if the project phases out."[2] Not only did she receive the financial resources, but she also found support from others, making the project sustainable and multiplying. As I heard her story, I thought of the women at St. Peter's on the other side of the world who supported one another through all the challenges and joys in their lives. Fyness and our women were caught together in a current of goodness, strengthened, empowered, and given new life.

In 2012, ELCA World Hunger committed not only to feeding hungry people but also to ensuring people had access to clean water. That year, financial gifts, including ours from St. Peter's, were sent to a small village called Niem in the dry western plains of the Central African Republic. The town of Niem, with a population of 10,000, had only two wells, but both were broken. The women and girls tasked with getting water for drinking, cooking, and washing had to retrieve dirty water from ponds, streams, or natural springs contaminated by animal and agricultural waste. Without access to clean water, people in Niem were often sick. In the Central African Republic at the time, one in four children died before they were five years old, many from waterborne diseases.[3]

However, in 2012, in partnership with Lutherans in the Central African Republic, the town of Niem received funding to build a spring box, a simple and inexpensive solution to the problem of contaminated water. A concrete box encloses a spring, with a pipe built into one side, allowing people to fill containers. Local people can install and maintain these

2 Cumming, *End Hunger?*, para. 8.

3 Evangelical Lutheran Church in America, *DIKO Marie's Story, 02:26.*

spring boxes, providing clean water for people that lasts. One of the people who benefited from this spring box was a fourteen-year-old girl named DIKO Marie. She said, "When the new spring box came, we no longer got sick because the water became clean and was safe to drink. Now the water is very clean. Before, we had to wait in line to get bad water. But now we do not have to wait. We can go home and continue with other activities . . . People were so happy when the spring box was done. Many people danced for joy."[4]

The prophet Isaiah was well-acquainted with the significance of water and the necessity of a provider. The prophet spoke to people who had long been in exile. They watched the Babylonians destroy their temple and city. Torn from their families and forced to live in a strange land, many of them lost their faith in a loving and present God. Yet, Isaiah held fast to his trust in God's faithfulness, envisioning that God would do what God had always done: bring freedom, healing, and restoration. Just as the rain came down from heaven, nourishing seeds and feeding the world, so too does God bring life to the world. "It will not return to me empty but will accomplish what I desire and achieve the purpose for which I sent it" (Isaiah 55:11).

God is faithful, making the soil rich and watering our seeds until they burst forth and sprout. The seeds of hope that the people of St. Peter's had sown were finally bursting forth with new life. The gifts we long dreamed of giving were now blessing people we'd never met but with whom we were linked by God's persistent current of love. The water, goodness, resources, generosity, and grace flowed with velocity and strength.

EPES

We made another significant legacy gift to Educación Popular en Salud (EPES), the healthcare ministry that St. Peter's had supported for years. In January 2012, the people of St. Peter's, through the legacy disbursement, gave $30,000 to EPES. In a lovely bit of holy serendipity, the gift came on the 30th Anniversary of EPES—$30,000 in their 30th year. Despite being their anniversary year, the organization had faced a tough financial year, and the timing could not have been better. The founder of EPES, Karen Anderson, described how they used our gift in an email to me.

4 Evangelical Lutheran Church in America, *DIKO Marie's Story*, 03:35–06:18.

For our 30th anniversary in 2012, we wanted to not only celebrate but also expand and deepen our work by providing training and small grants to community groups throughout Chile. We held trainings in the far north, the south, and in Santiago for 43 community groups to collectively work on assessments of health priorities in each region. In the three meetings, a long list of local problems was identified, including a lack of mental health services, shelters for women victims of violence, and the overall absence of a preventive approach to community health.

In response, EPES organized a Community Project Fund that awarded small grants to 14 community groups to conduct their own community health projects. The projects included: freedom from violence workshops with families in emergency housing after the earthquake, activities to protect disappearing wetlands, sex education with youth in Chile's largest shantytown, a clean-up of abandoned common areas near a Lutheran pre-school in a poor area, and others. The idea was also that, along with the funds, we would provide technical assistance to smaller organizations regarding project writing, budgeting, and reporting that could strengthen their overall work in the future.

The gift from St. Peter's helped fund the workshops and the small grants that educated and mobilized hundreds of people throughout Chile. We were profoundly grateful for this gift that came to EPES at such a key moment and helped make our anniversary year not just a celebration but a time of expanding our mission and supporting many community health initiatives.

SEMINARY SCHOLARSHIPS

The largest of our legacy gifts went to Gettysburg Seminary to help fund scholarships for people studying for ministry. Seminaries nationwide struggle to continue their essential work with fewer resources and support. In a creative and faithful response to these challenges, the two Pennsylvania ELCA seminaries merged in 2017. Now known as United Lutheran Seminary, the institution retains two campuses, located in Gettysburg and Philadelphia. When I learned of the unification of the two seminaries, I rejoiced not only in the continuation of these schools but also because it offered a sort of healing resolution. After that bitter dispute about where our scholarship money would go, there was a kind of mending from knowing that in the end, the money went to both. In the end, no one lost.

Students who received scholarships from St. Peter's now serve in a vast array of ministries. Their stories represent the beautiful diversity of the Lutheran Church, not just in the United States but worldwide. Several students serve as parish pastors, with many located on the Eastern seaboard. Our scholarship money enabled them to study and helped them step into parish ministry without the weight of debt, offering them the freedom to accept calls in smaller congregations or into often-forgotten neighborhoods.

Some of those students who benefited directly from St. Peter's scholarship support began in congregations but now serve the church and world in various ways. One leads our denomination in our anti-racism efforts and supports leaders of color. Another serves a congregation as a community organizer, building powerful relationships that respond to the needs of their neighbors, particularly LGBTQ and other marginalized people. One pastor preaches on Sundays, but for most of the week, he tends to a small farm that provides good, healthy food for those who need it while stewarding the soil well.

Ashrouf Tannous, a Palestinian pastor serving in Bethlehem, found his calling after a friend encouraged him to consider studies at United Seminary. Before long, Tannous was enrolled in the Doctor of Ministry program at United, completing coursework while raising his young family in the West Bank. None of this would've been possible, and the debt would've been insurmountable, were it not for scholarship gifts like those St. Peter's was able to provide. When I talked to him on Zoom, his three sons did their own zooming in and out of the screen. It was evening, and his wife was out shopping for Christmas. We talked in December of 2024; Pastor Tannous, his family, his congregation, and his neighbors were living through the uncertainty, violence, and war between Hamas and Israel.

He shared the life and vibrancy of the ministry of the Evangelical Lutheran Church of Jerusalem and the Holy Land (ELCJHL) and the work they do to provide care, nurture, and support for the people, more important now than ever. Along with running hospitals and schools, the church provides critical assistance to refugees living in the West Bank. Tannous made clear that many more young adults have a yearning to do ministry in the West Bank, but that their aspirations are reliant on global partnerships and scholarships of the variety that St. Peter's helped make possible.

Pastor Tannous asked me to keep praying for them all, and specifically, he wanted time to write. He had to delay finishing his doctoral work because of the violence and turmoil throughout Gaza, Israel, and the West

Bank following October 7, 2023. The leaders of the church had an increased demand for caring for their people in a time of war, with the unknowns of their future, the increased violence in the West Bank, and all the repercussions in that community. They also had to keep telling their story to the world to ensure they were not forgotten and that the lives of Muslim and Christian Palestinians, both in Gaza and the West Bank, would not be abandoned.

Pastor Tannous is a figure worth getting to know. "I pray that there will be enough people to shout and be the voice of the voiceless," he said in one 2023 interview. "I pray for mercy. I pray as Jesus said: Blessed are the peacemakers, because they will be called the children of God. I pray that the whole world would recognize us as Palestinians here. That we are the descendants of Jesus. We are the people of this land. I pray that peace may prevail. I pray that love may prevail. And I pray that people may feel our suffering and act accordingly."[5]

After bone-wearying days of pastoral and prophetic work, then time as a dad with baths, games, and stories, Pastor Tannous didn't have the energy to study or write. The loss the Palestinian people have experienced because of war, occupation, and violence cannot be overstated. So many thousands of lives have been cut short, families torn apart, homes buried in rubble, and entire communities destroyed. But other human needs and joys are lost, too. The loss of the ability and freedom to ride a bike through the countryside, to tend to the family olive grove, to get to church (and to work, or to visit family) without going through checkpoints, to live without the daily theft of dignity, freedom, and agency. And, for one pastor, in addition to all the other devastation, the violence and uncertainty have taken away the time and space to write, to study. In comparison, it might seem small, but it is significant, not just for Pastor Tannous, but for the global Church.

NEW JERSEY FUND FOR MISSION

Another legacy gift from St. Peter's was given to the New Jersey Synod's Fund for Mission. Every year, investment income from this fund is distributed to congregations throughout New Jersey to support special mission needs. Over the years, thousands of dollars have supported creative and thoughtful ministries that respond to the needs of neighbors and strengthen congregations. The legacy gift of St. Peter's increased the value of that fund

5. Dueuck, "Palestinian Christian Leaders," para. 13.

so that the committee could share even more with new mission ventures, with a priority for projects that reflect the Synod's core value of diversity and that address the needs of the disadvantaged, especially people living in poverty, those with mental and physical challenges, and the powerless.

One of the Fund for Mission grant recipients has been the Lunchtime Ministry of St. Matthew-Trinity Lutheran Church in Hoboken. This ministry provides breakfast and lunch every day to hungry people. But it's so much more than just food. Volunteers create a space for relationships and belonging, where social service providers can make connections, offer art and guitar lessons, and provide a closet full of hygiene supplies and socks, along with many other resources for people.

It all began in the 1970s when the older women of the then primarily German community met regularly to make quilts and knit blankets for the homeless people in the neighborhood. The women crafted, drank coffee, and ate a simple lunch and snacks. Soon, others joined them, and they realized that the new quilters came more for the sandwiches and warm coffee than for the sewing. At the time, and still today, many senior citizens experience food insecurity as they try to juggle housing costs, medical expenses, and food. Soon, quilters became chefs. The ministry has grown to the point where 60–80 people sit down and eat each day. Around tables, with hot coffee served all morning, friendships and community grow. As one of the leaders said, "The guests are not our guests. They are brothers and sisters."

The Fund for Mission also gave grants to support the ministry of Santa Isabel Lutheran Church in Elizabeth, New Jersey. Santa Isabel has two worshipping communities. One congregation worships in a large, beautiful old brick church tucked into a diverse residential neighborhood of Elizabeth. The other assembles for worship inside the Elizabeth Detention Center, a U.S. Immigration and Customs Enforcement contract facility operated by the for-profit company CoreCivic. In October of 2024, 285 immigrants were detained there, with authorities planning to add up to 600 more people to their population.[6] Most of the detainees held have fled to the United States from violence in their home countries, only to find themselves stuck in a slow justice system and the inhumane conditions of this detention center.[7]

The leaders from Santa Isabel draw their inspiration for worshipping among ICE detainees from none other than Jesus, who said: "I was in prison and you visited me." In English and Spanish, they sing hymns, study

6 Levine, "ICE Could Add 600 Beds."

7 Katz, "ICE Jailer in New Jersey."

scripture, and share bread and wine. Along with other members of San Isabel and often other Lutheran advocates and friends, the congregation behind bars finds sustenance, community, and support. They are reminded that despite all the harsh and inhumane treatment, they are, indeed, beloved children of God and siblings in Christ, and not forgotten.

In these and so many other ways, devoted people of faith have a way of showing up in love for their neighbors. While our church in North Plainfield may have come to an end, the faithful witness of the Church cannot be stopped. Creative and life-giving ministries throughout New Jersey have been established and continue to be sustained by grants from the Fund for Mission. Thanks to Lutheran communities throughout New Jersey, people without homes now have access to shelter, rental assistance, and advocacy. Congregations from the mountains in North Jersey to the shores in South Jersey to the urban suburbs around New York City and Philadelphia are feeding hungry people through food pantries, school backpacks full of food for weekends, and community gardens.

The gifts given within New Jersey not only reached our neighbors outside the walls of the church, but also those sitting and singing in the pews. In appreciation for our organist, Julie, and the many musicians who have served at St. Peter's over the years, a legacy gift was made to the New Jersey Synod to establish a fund that supports individuals interested in pursuing a career as a church musician. The idea was to help cover the cost of organ or piano lessons for individuals who would utilize those skills to lead worship. This fund has supported the training of gifted musicians for the church, but congregations have also utilized the grant for creative programs. One community in Morrisville, Pennsylvania, comprised primarily of Liberian families, received a grant to provide children with piano lessons. These lessons blessed their worship life and provided personal growth and enhancement to students who would not otherwise have access to that musical education.

All over the world, from Chile to Malawi, from the Central African Republic to Bethlehem, and within congregations all over the United States, people have been impacted by the generosity of the people of St. Peter's Lutheran Church in North Plainfield. As Isaiah promised, the rain came down from heaven, flowing out to the world, doing that for which God gave it purpose. I'll never forget my friend Grace saying to me in the church hallway years ago, "We know what it means to be the church; we just can't do it anymore." However, through our generous gifts in the world, the community of St. Peter's has helped the church continue to be the church.

Our faithfulness and compassion live on through the people and lives we've impacted.

22

2009-PRESENT

Ascension

And Jesus came and said to them, "All authority in heaven and on earth has been given to me. Go therefore and make disciples of all nations, baptizing them in the name of the Father and of the Son and of the Holy Spirit and teaching them to obey everything that I have commanded you. And remember, I am with you always, to the end of the age" (Matthew 28:17–20).

BACK IN JUNE OF 2009, soon after the members of St. Peter's voted to close, we included some words from Amy in a letter sent to the congregation. Amy shared her disappointment and experienced an internal forgiveness during communion. Her reflections gave comfort and hope to our people. She wrote:

> One meaningful way in which we might view our future is to use the analogy of the homeless program that was once hosted for many years here at St. Peter's. Our move will be like that, only turned on its head. We will be the "homeless" as we leave St. Peter's behind. As we make the difficult decision to transfer to another Lutheran church, that church will become a safe haven for us, much in the same way that St. Peter's was for so many guests for so many years, guests who needed a place to rest, a place to sort

> things out, a place to plan and decide their future, a place to begin again.
>
> We will all have been given the blessing of time, and a little space, and a little breathing room, to come to understand into what future God is calling each one of us, while all the while, there will be shepherding, pastoral care, and the sympathy and understanding of new friends, all which will be very much needed at this critical time. "Blest Be the Tie that Binds . . . " as we sang in church on a recent Sunday. For our St. Peter's congregation, there could not be a more appropriate hymn.

I have lost track of many of our people since our closing. I don't know the continuation of everyone's stories. For better or worse, distance and the passage of time cause one to miss out on lives that change and evolve. But from what I can glean, Amy's prayerful hope became a reality for many of our people. It did take a little time, with some space for breathing, for us to understand the shape of the future to which God called us. As time and distance pulled us from one another, I prayed for our people but knew little about their lives and well-being beyond a periodic Christmas card. I trusted that God would care for the ones I kept on loving in God's own surprising way.

GRACE

In the fall of 2013, I learned that Grace had died. She and Roy had moved to a retirement home in Pennsylvania to be closer to one of their sons, though they retained their connection to their community of faith in New Jersey. My heart broke for Roy, their sons and grandkids, and all of us who love Grace. I remembered the conversations we had before St. Peter's closed and her deep fear that no one could share her story after she died.

The people of St. Stephen's gave Grace a fitting send-off. The new pastor at St. Stephen's preached her funeral sermon, honoring Grace's depth of faith. He told the story that whenever her choir mates started to get off tune, they would lean in, close to Grace, to get into tune again. Then Pastor Chris said this:

> And, at that great choral consummation before the throne of God, which we read about in the Book of Revelation . . . When we all sing together, "Blessing and glory and wisdom and thanksgiving and honor and power and might be to God forever and ever." When we sing of hungering no more, of a cool shelter and a gentle

> spring—when we sing of God wiping away every tear. When we sing this song together, I believe you will see a section of that heavenly host leaning toward Grace to make sure they're in tune as they sing to their Savior and hers.[1]

It brought me joy to think of Grace forever singing those songs of hope. Even after her death, her deep trust and bigheartedness continue to shape the lives of so many of us.

KATHERINE

Years later, Katherine reminisced about her days leaning in to sing alongside Grace. Katherine and I were walking along the beach on Long Beach Island, down the Jersey Shore. In the years after Charlie's death, it had become a tradition for her family to spend a week down the Jersey Shore. Katherine rented a house and spent the week with her sons and their families. I made a trip back to New Jersey to reconnect with some of our members, hear their stories, and learn how God had shown up for them since St. Peter's closing. Part of me hoped to meet Katherine in her familiar house in North Plainfield, where Charlie's glass bottle collection remained, her tea kettle was always on, and I could see the pictures of Charlie and her family, which filled the flowered, wallpapered walls.

Instead, we met on a rainy summer day at a rental home just a block from the Atlantic Ocean. As the rain fell, we ate sandwiches and shared stories, catching up on our lives. Her son, daughter-in-law, and their teenage kids delightfully interrupted our conversation. Katherine spoke with her trademark honesty, speaking of past years' challenges and goodness. Like always, she was quick to tears and just as fast to laughter.

Along with others, Katherine had joined St. Stephen's and jumped into ministry. She told me about Hilda using the quilters as a place for the two congregations to find shared purpose and friendship. Her funeral was one of the first after St. Peter's closed. After her death, Hilda's husband Anders made a home in the kitchen at the new church, cooking and serving at the counter whenever the congregation hosted community meals. I thought about Hilda, mourned not only by the people of St. Peter's but also by the people of St. Stephen's, who came to be blessed by Hilda's good humor,

1 Halverson, "Evelyn Troy Funeral Sermon."

generosity as enormous as she was tall, and her knowledge of German swear words.

As Katherine and I remembered these saints, I envisioned Hilda and Grace keeping company in heaven, delighting in their renewed companionship. I wondered if Hilda would be singing in that choir of angels, leaning close to match Grace's beautiful tone. Someday, I'll find out, but for now, I'm convinced Hilda is delighting in the company of the ones she loves, swearing up a storm, making even her Savior laugh.

Katherine shared how the pastor at St. Stephen's tapped her and Clara to be on the stewardship committee early in her time at St. Stephen's. They didn't just focus on raising money but on finding ways to create deeper community and connections. During Lent, they had the idea of inviting people to become prayer partners. Members of the congregation pulled a heart-shaped piece of paper from a basket with someone else's name on it. They connected with that person to pray with and for over the season of Lent. They tried to be intentional about forming partnerships with people who didn't already know one another, in hopes of building a deeper community and creating new connections. Katherine talked about how she had just served as the chair of the call committee at St. Stephen's when they called their latest pastor. With a catch in her voice, she talked about how it was a way she could honor and remember Charlie, who had chaired my call committee.

As she always did, Katherine held deep joy and sadness together in her heart. She missed Charlie deeply but kept finding ways to live forward, passing on his goodness and wisdom to her kids, living in her own generous and faithful ways. Even as she missed the people and community at St. Peter's, this didn't stop her from investing her whole self in a new congregation.

The transition into belonging to a new congregation isn't always easy. People must compromise and work through frustrations and unmet expectations, much like blended families do. The rituals and practices of a new congregation can seem strange and peculiar at first, and may even be intimidating or off-putting. But the people of St. Stephen's were gracious and flexible, finding ways to open themselves to the ideas and presence of new people. Katherine had found a place where she could serve in leadership and find communal support, echoing the legacy of her beloved husband.

As Katherine and I talked, the sun broke through the clouds, and we decided to walk further along the beach. Both of us had aged a bit over the dozen years since we'd been together in North Plainfield, spending hours together writing letters, discussing plans and leadership, and caring for our people. With more gray hair now and a few new aches in our bodies, our lives had taken lots of turns. We had plenty of grief to assess, but more than enough hope and new life to compensate.

Thanks to the rain that morning, the beach was unusually empty for a July day. We talked through the joys and losses of our lives, the now sainted people who mattered to us, and the forward nature of life. The sound of the waves breaking on the beach and the briny smell of the ocean only added to the scope of our laughter and tears. I thought of one of Isak Dinesen's *Gothic Tales*, where a young man named Jonathon, prone to melancholy, asks the Cardinal:

> "Do you know a cure for me?"
>
> "Why yes," the Cardinal said, "I know a cure for everything: salt water."
>
> "Salt water?" I asked him.
>
> "Yes," he said, "in one way or the other. Sweat, or tears, or the salt sea."[2]

To me, Katherine is (and always has been) a living testimony of the way in which salt water heals. She works up a sweat in living her commitments to others, feeding hungry people, tending to the needs of those around her, and still thinking of ways to care for kids at the school where she once worked. Whenever she remembers with gratitude the people she has loved, and whose death now leaves a void in her days, her tears flow freely. Our walk before the broad horizon of the Atlantic Ocean, in the visceral presence of God's love, wonder, and breadth, was just what we needed. Sweat, tears, and the sea are just what heals.

JILL

Earlier that week, I spent an evening at a classic New Jersey Diner with Clara, Jill, and Debbie, other St. Peter's people from my past. I heard about their families, adventures, and challenges over the years, and shared about my own. We talked about our last months at St. Peter's and all that has transpired over the past decade.

2 Dinesen, *Seven Gothic Tales*, 39.

Over grilled sandwiches and omelets as big as our plates, we laughed and got a little weepy. Jill, as she often did, talked the most. Now in her 70s, with the same curly hair and broad smile, she walked more slowly on aging knees. Jill's children grew up alongside Katherine's boys at St. Peter's. Her husband died far too early, just months after Charlie. In the months leading up to our closing, Jill had stepped into leadership on the council, a role she had avoided for years. However, in doing so, she discovered she had a knack for leadership. In the years to come, this proved to be the case.

Jill settled well into ministry at St. Stephen's. She started writing birthday cards to members and serving in whatever way she could. It helped that a group from St. Peter's moved to St. Stephen's together. A few familiar faces in a new place never hurt for finding one's way. Jill laughed at how, months after our closing, the money counters at St. Stephen's still had to deal with processing checks written to "St. Peter's Lutheran Church." It is hard to change our habits.

Everyone seemed to have indelible memories from the COVID years and how those months of lockdown had impacted them and their congregations. Jill had been a member of the church council at the time. During that time, she kept thinking about St. Peter's ministry for the homeless and our call as Christians to respond to the needs of the poor. The whole idea of a drive-thru food pantry was entirely Jill's.

So, from then on, to this day, every other week, Jill organizes people to collect and pack up whatever food, household supplies, and diapers they can find. People set up tables and spend the afternoon outside as people drive through the parking lot at St. Stephen's, receiving food boxes. After seeing her neighbors' need, all Jill could do was respond with the leadership she once doubted.

CLARA

As I might have predicted, Clara jumped fully into life at St. Stephen's. Having moved around a lot in her career as a nurse, she had practice in starting anew in a community of faith. Clara's circle of hair that surrounded her face, full of wrinkles from a lifetime of smiles, had gone completely white. While her mind was as sharp as ever, her voice was quieter than I remembered. Clara had aged, but remained as wise and grounded in faith as ever.

At one point in our conversation, she handed me a book, *Seeing with the Mind, Hearing with the Heart: A Thematic Bible Study on the Gospel of*

Luke by a Young Pastor and a Not-So-Young Parishioner. I had heard about this book she had written with the pastor from St. Stephen's, but I hadn't picked up a copy yet. Later, I devoured it, grateful to be blessed again by Clara's wisdom and deep faith. In the introduction, Clara describes herself as "not a minister or Bible scholar, but someone who, through fifty years of life as a nurse, a teacher, and a regular churchgoer, has tried to be faithful to the practice of daily Bible reading. Whether it has been in my cozy 'devotions' chair with my morning coffee or under the covers with a flashlight on a cot in the Saudi desert, the Bible has been my daily companion. Always God speaks to me through his Word . . . So grab your favorite Bible translation . . . I switch off between the NRSV, the NIV, "The Message," and the Amplified Version within easy reach."[3]

I smiled at the end of this passage, remembering the study with our women at St. Peter's and how Clara would always spread her many Bibles around her. With a lifetime rooted in God's word and listening, Clara had found ways to use her gifts at St. Stephen's. She led Bible Studies and visited homebound members. With Katherine, she helped to steward not only the financial giving of the church but also some of the spiritual practices of the congregation.

Listening to the stories of these women around that table in the diner, I gave thanks for what God had done in and through them. Each of these servants was a specialist in finding unexpected and beautiful ways to spark new life in me and in others. But I knew that not all the people of St. Peter's had experienced this. Some of the people I had hoped to meet while I visited New Jersey didn't respond or didn't want to see me. I don't know all the reasons, but some had just moved on, and others still carried wounds from our ending. There were others whom I just couldn't track down.

DEBBIE

During my trip to New Jersey, I met up with Debbie for breakfast. While the waitress kept pouring coffee into cups, she caught me up on her son Ethan, once an acolyte but now making music and writing books. Debbie had grown up at St. Peter's. Her grandparents were pillars of the congregation, and her dad had been the Sunday School superintendent decades ago. She'd be the first to say that nothing formed her faith as consequentially as the congregation giving shape to her spirit over the years. Before becoming

3 Halverson and Nietman, *Seeing with the Mind,* viii-ix.

a teacher, she worked in youth ministry and other professional church activities in her early life. Debbie's family lived west of North Plainfield, but she never hesitated to drive the thirty minutes to church over the years. The distance didn't feel long because of how the community had shaped her, how they loved her son, and because of her long history with the congregation.

However, when St. Peter's closed, she looked for a community of faith closer to home and found her way to Living Waters Lutheran Church. Debbie took her time easing in, worshiping unobtrusively and without fanfare, simply comforted by enjoying the piano that once belonged to St. Peter's. She discovered that people she had known over the years were there, and she found new friendships. It became an increasingly good fit, though it was hard to let go of what was and claim a new place as home.

Living Waters had just moved into their new building. The mortgage debt burden of their beautiful facility, however, added significant stress to trying to meet even their most basic furnishing needs. So, when St. Peter's gave them its piano, altar paraments, and more, these were like gifts from heaven. The congregation tried to be good stewards, installing solar panels and designing the roof's slope to block out the sun in the summer and let in light when the winter sun is low. The gift of dishes from St. Peter's meant they would no longer have to buy or throw away disposable cups.

After worshiping with the people at Living Waters for a while, Debbie finally decided that the time had come to join the new congregation. She didn't take this decision lightly, but with a mix of grief about what had been lost and hope for what would come. After worship, the congregation celebrated their newest members with cake and coffee. While they chatted and ate, Debbie pulled aside a few people who were important to her. She walked with them into the sanctuary and over to the baptismal font.

This font is as unique, artistic, and dynamic as a congregation called Living Waters needs it to be. A large metal bowl, thick and strong, sits atop a hammered pedestal anchored by a base filled with river rocks. Nearby is a water wall made of clear glass, bringing the sight and sound of flowing, living water into the worship space. The day Debbie joined, she went to that font and pulled the small rock I had given her on the morning of St. Peter's closing out of her pocket. She had been carrying it around for months, holding onto it, remembering the saints who had been her rock, hoping in the power of the resurrection, and the stone rolled away from the tomb. Debbie knelt at the foot of the font as the sound of flowing water whispered with assurance around her. She placed her rock among the river rocks at the foundation of Living Water's baptismal font.

The beauty of one stone mixed in with a host of others is the indistinguishability of that one over time. Debbie had no way of knowing which underwater stone was hers, or where that representation of her life sat among the other saints. Nor did it matter. She had found her place there among the river rocks of Living Waters. While she still carried the grief of St. Peter's ending and the disconnection from the history she had known, Debbie no longer had to bear the weight of that rock. A new community welcomed her warmly. She started to sing in the choir, which she had never been able to do at St. Peter's because it was too hard to get to rehearsals midweek. Over the years, the congregation tapped her to be council president, teach Sunday School, and host a Christmas cookie exchange. When it is her turn, Debbie takes responsibility for ironing the white, fair linen, the delicate and precious tablecloth on their altar, the same fair linen she had ironed and seen for decades on the altar at St. Peter's.

Finding a home in a new faith community takes time. It is impossible to replace a web of relationships that has been spun over decades in just a few weeks. We cannot immediately re-create a sense of familiarity in a place or patterns of worship. It takes committing to the awkward, hard months. Beginning in a new community is like stepping into a zero-entry pool, starting in the shallow end with small talk and cautious connecting, but moving into the deeper end as trust is built. Some people have the courage or personality to jump in all at once, but even then, it takes commitment to stay in the water. Belonging demands openness and sticking around. It's a whole mix of compromising, giving, and taking. Even when we feel sadness and loss, we can feel the contradictory joy and delight in the new place all at the same time.

NANCY

As I tracked down different St. Peter's parishioners over the months and revisited all kinds of memories with them, I found Nancy in Phoenix, Arizona. We met at the Desert Botanical Gardens. She raised her kids alongside Jill and Katherine and sang in the choir. Like most people in small congregations, she did a little of every job needed to make a church run. She would often host a congregational Christmas party at her old home just a few blocks from St. Peter's. George would walk around with a pitcher of Manhattans, and the Anders ensured we had plenty of Norwegian cookies. Just before St. Peter's closed, Nancy and her husband moved down the shore to live in South Jersey, closer to one of their kids. After her husband's death, Nancy moved to Arizona.

We walked around the varieties of cacti and artfully arranged succulents. I caught up on Nancy's life over the past decade. She carried the sadness of her husband's death, and the ways life continues, full of joy and purpose. Mostly, though, we reminisced about the people of St. Peter's and the ways they blessed us, even after their death, even when we were no longer together.

Before we left, Nancy told me she had something to give me, and I walked with her to her car. She pulled a bag of perfectly ripe grapefruit out of her back seat. People all over the Phoenix area have citrus trees in their yards, but the fruit often rots because people can't eat all the fruit those trees produce. With others in her congregation, Nancy gleans fruit from suburban yards and then distributes it to shelters, soup kitchens, and anyone who needs it, including a former pastor soaking up the sunshine and company as a reprieve from February in Iowa. With the same spirit of generosity, she lived in New Jersey, but in a new place and way. Nancy responds with love to those who need it.

Near the front of the sanctuary at St. Peter's is an Ascension Window. The colored glass depicts Jesus in a white robe, his arms up like a referee at a football game signaling a successful field goal. Jesus lifts up from the ground, floating, one bare foot exposed, the other tucked behind him under his floating robe. With a peaceful, almost dazed look, Jesus gazes down at the earth.

The windows around the sanctuary narrate the life story of Jesus, but they skip right from the crucifixion window to the ascension window. Given the limited space, it makes sense that they chose not to depict any of the post-Easter stories. The resurrection appearances were quieter and often mysterious. Only Mary Magdalene saw Jesus at the tomb and initially mistook him for the gardener. Jesus walked with his friends along the road to Emmaus, and they hardly recognized him. None of these appearances were particularly glorious, shiny, or golden. Jesus met them where they were, on the road, on the beach at dawn, while they were locked up in fear.

Jesus' resurrection power often comes in seemingly mundane moments of restoration. A rock in a baptismal font. An invitation to serve on the church council. A song that echoes back to people. A walk along the beach. A meal at a New Jersey diner. A bag of grapefruit. A question about names on stained glass windows. A mailman who ended up in an obituary. A prayer partner chosen from a hat. God's way of bringing us new life and pulling us through our grief usually happens in small ways.

The newly resurrected Jesus never encouraged his followers to sit back and bask in some unexpected glory. He put them to work immediately, giving them a rather large assignment. He told his friends, "Go to the ends of the earth and share my love with the world. The Holy Spirit will be with you. Go, now, to make it known." This is Jesus unmistakably passing the baton to those who knew him best. He tells them to go and spread the good news, to leave the comfort of their small community, and to be the people God made them to be. "Now, you are in charge," Jesus says as he floats to heaven. "It is your turn now."

The disciples surely missed the comfort and the familiarity of their friends, with Jesus among them. They must have mourned the loss of their companion: his humor, his stories, his strength, his love. For those first followers, stepping into new beginnings was more than just awkward; it was dangerous, full of impossibilities, and fraught with persecutions. But they stepped out, courageously telling the story of Jesus everywhere, from Rome to India, and from Turkey to Ethiopia.

The people of St. Peter's stepped up and out, too. Our once tight-knit community now lives and worships throughout New Jersey, Arizona, Pennsylvania, North Carolina, Iowa, and beyond. Our resources have been sprinkled around the world. The more former parishioners I meet, the more convinced I am that each of us is doing our best to share the goodness and love of Jesus.

Our supper at the diner eventually came to an end. As I tucked a black and white cookie into my purse, I posed a question to the group that I had been waiting all evening to ask: "Do any of you regret our decision to close?" I could see them thinking quickly, so I jumped in with a clarification to my own question: "Do any of you believe we made a mistake?" Each one of them shook their heads. They named how hard it was, how challenging the conversations were, how people spoke their minds, and how we made the decision together. They spoke about how grateful they were for the people, many of whom are now living in eternal joy with God. They shared how proud they were that the congregation never stopped making our financial commitments to the larger church and our mission partners, giving themselves away until the end.

Debbie seemed to speak for the whole group. "We did the right thing at the right time. It was not an individual decision, but all of us together. We didn't wait until we were without money, and, fortunately, we were wise enough not to hold on until there were only three people left. We didn't hold on for dear life. Instead, we prayerfully considered what to do, and we did it. It wasn't easy. We had a long history. But it was the right thing for us."

23

2023

Thomas

A week later, Jesus' disciples were again in the house, and Thomas was with them. Although the doors were shut, Jesus came and stood among them and said, "Peace be with you." Then he said to Thomas, "Put your finger here and see my hands. Reach out your hand and put it in my side. Do not doubt but believe" (John 20:24–29).

Nearly fourteen years had passed before I returned to that familiar brick church building on the corner of Grove and Mercer streets in North Plainfield. From the outside, the building looked mostly the same. The backyard, with its enormous tree, had been turned into a much-needed parking lot, but my favorite, cathedral-shaped, red wooden doors on the side of the building were still there, with their fish-imprinted metal door handles. I arrived early for my meeting with the building's new residents, so I walked around outside and noticed how well they were taking care of it. I admired the new windows and roof, the grass and bushes trimmed. The sign no longer said, "St. Peter's Lutheran Church," but instead, "Saints Basilios-Gregorios Orthodox Church."

For a long while, our building had sat empty. It entered the market in 2009, when the stock market crashed, and the real estate bubble burst. We couldn't have picked a worse time to put a building up for sale. Roy, George, and others kept an eye on the building while the synod treasurer showed the space, answered questions, and worked with potential buyers. Months and then years went by as nothing happened. In many places, former church buildings are transformed into unique condos, artsy restaurants, or unconventional Airbnbs. These are necessary and good ways to repurpose church buildings. But the people of St. Peter's hoped the building would remain a house of worship.

As that building remained unused for some years, I know the former congregational leaders were caught in this in-between space, unable to move forward fully. I never doubted we made the right decision, but I questioned my own words about how God would bring a new future to us and through us. How would God plant new seeds through our legacy hopes if the resources remained stuck in an unsold building?

We were hardly alone in asking these questions. Doubt has been woven into the experience of faithful people from the very beginning. When she heard that she'd have a son as a wrinkled, aging woman, Sarah's doubt came out as laughter. Moses questioned whether God could work through a stutterer like him, and the doubts of the Israelites echoed across the wilderness as they wondered if they'd ever reach that promised land. A man whose son was possessed by a spirit said to Jesus, "I believe, help my unbelief." When his friends stood with Jesus on the mountain after the resurrection, "they worshiped him, but some doubted."

Jesus' friend Thomas remains the champion of these doubters. But if we put ourselves in Thomas's shoes (sandals?), we can sympathize with why he asked his question. After giving his life to follow Jesus, Thomas watched his friend and hope for the universe die on the cross. A few days later, Thomas wasn't with the others locked in the upper room when the risen Christ appeared. He refused to believe Jesus was alive until he saw it with his own eyes. But Jesus returned and said to Thomas, "Here, look at my hands. Feel the wounds on my side."

Jesus never shamed Thomas' doubt, but he also said, "Blessed are those who have not seen, and yet believe." Those of us on this side of the ascension are among those who believe without seeing. And yet, even though we haven't seen the actual body of the risen Jesus, the Body of Christ still shows up for us in ways we can see, hear, touch, and feel today. We hear Him in the community that sings with us when our own voice falters, feel Him in the hands of people who show up when we are drowning, and see Him in people who tend to an empty building. And I heard this word of realized resurrection in the news that St. Peter's building had been sold, the legacy gifts shared, and a new community had found a home in that small brick building we had loved.

After those days in the upper rooms with Jesus, the book of Acts recounts how the Spirit scattered Thomas and the other disciples to share the message of Jesus. Peter and his friends began the first churches in Jerusalem, initiating the spread of the Good News across the Roman Empire. Arrows on maps depict Paul's journeys around the Mediterranean Sea to Rome, beginning churches all along the way. Those communities of faith grew and flourished, building the foundation of what would become the Christian Church in Western Europe.

But the book of Acts and the letters of the New Testament don't contain the conclusion to all the stories, including what happened to Thomas. Just as Paul took the story of Jesus westward toward Rome, Thomas carried the message of Jesus eastward, across the Arabian Sea to India. Thomas is said to have established eight congregations in Kerala, on the western coast of India, baptizing many people and sharing the stories of Jesus.

Christians have been in Kerala and on the Indian subcontinent for centuries. Along with Hinduism, Islam, and other religions, Christianity thrives throughout India with a vast diversity of practice and theology. Through all the changes, as various generations and denominations of Christian missionaries came to India, Thomist Orthodox Christians held fast to their faith. They passed it on through generations and generations, developing a deep theological and liturgical tradition in common lineage and practice with Orthodox communities throughout the world.

Now, just as German immigrants had done a century before, generations of Indian immigrants have made a home in New Jersey. Among them is a community that traces their spiritual ancestry back to Thomas and the eight churches in Kerala. The congregation of Saints Basilios-Gregorios Orthodox Church had been worshiping in a chapel at Rutgers University, borrowing the space for a few hours a week. They were growing and running out of room, people in need of a sanctuary to call their own.

Families from this Orthodox congregation came from all over central New Jersey, generations of South Indian families who speak Malayalam, the language of Kerala (and the only language in the world that is also a palindrome). Reportedly, they looked at many buildings but kept returning to our little brick church in North Plainfield. The building had much to offer them; the sanctuary was beautiful and sacred, and the Fellowship Hall and kitchen were perfect for community meals and learning. So, they put an offer together and invested in that building, which became their spiritual home.

In 2023, I planned a trip to New Jersey to connect with some of our St. Peter's people, a time for diner meals and beach walks. I also wanted to make a visit to the brick church I had loved in North Plainfield. I reached out to Fr. Thomas, the vicar of the congregation, asking if I could meet him, walk through the building, and learn more about his congregation (the congregation he served). Graciously making time in his busy days. Fr. Thomas met me on the sidewalk outside the church. He was joined by Mr. P. K. Jacob, one of the senior members of the congregation and part of the Board of Trustees. Mr. Jacob, affectionately known by his church as Jacob Uncle, reminded me so much of Roy, with his quiet strength and commitment to his community. Like Roy, Mr. Jacob tended to the building, helping with renovations and maintenance.

The tour of the building started at the side door, with a fresh layer of red paint on the old wooden slats. It still stuck in the door frame, as it always did. Fr. Thomas apologized, saying that no matter how often they tried to fix it, it never quite fit. But they loved the old door and just decided to live with its imperfection. I laughed and said the same had been true for decades. I walked inside as they tugged at the door to make sure it closed. Even if I had been blindfolded, I would have known where I stood. The building smelled the same. They showed me the offices, which had the same warm glow of the colored glass in the windows, the same aging wood paneling. Piles of books, written in Malayalam and English, filled the shelves in the pastor's study.

They were excited to show me how they had updated the bathrooms to make them accessible. The Fellowship Hall had also been renovated, featuring new flooring, lighting, screens, and other learning technologies. The child-sized wooden chairs we had left in the building were arranged in neat rows in the Sunday School rooms. New lessons were written on the chalkboards, though you could still see the layers of words from generations of learning and games.

As we toured the building, I asked about their congregation. Their Sunday school had over a hundred children, and dozens of families from all over central New Jersey made their way to worship each week. Many were second and third-generation immigrants, carrying on the traditions and faith of their ancestors. They had language lessons in the Fellowship Hall, large meals, classes, service projects, and social gatherings. The space was as much of a cultural center as a church. Like it had been for generations before, the building was a place where friendships, faith, and generosity grew.

They were very curious about the shower in the Sunday School bathroom. I explained how St. Peter's had been part of a rotating shelter for people without homes, and that it was installed as part of the hospitality for the families who slept overnight. I shared stories about the generosity of the people, the restoration of the fire and pews, various building projects over the years, and the meals, variety shows, and learning in the Fellowship Hall. With joy, Fr. Thomas showed me the air conditioning unit they added, "I don't know how you made it through all those hot summers without cool air!"

As we walked up the stairs toward the main door to the sanctuary, Fr. Thomas and Mr. Jacob stepped out of their shoes. He graciously nodded to me and said, "We take off our shoes inside the sanctuary. Out of respect. It is holy ground." I slid my shoes off. As we stepped toward the sanctuary doors next to the Good Samaritan window, the horse as blue as ever, Fr. Thomas stopped me, "Just to warn you, we've changed a lot. It will look a lot different." He seemed nervous, worried perhaps that I'd react negatively to changes made, but he was also proud and wanted me to love it as much as they did.

As they opened the door and we walked down the center aisle, the renewed beauty of the space astounded me. The front of the sanctuary no longer had the high wooden pulpit, and they removed the screened corner that held the organ speakers. In their place hung warm, regal, red velvet curtains to conceal the altar. The formerly blocked walls had been drywalled and finished to a smooth, clean surface, painted a warm cream, with gold trim around the arches. Beautiful icons filled the empty spaces of the walls.

So much also remained the same. Exposed wood beams held the high ceiling. The worn dark wood pews, refinished after the 1940s fire, were freshly polished. The windows, telling the story of Jesus, still surrounded us. The soft red carpet still led down the aisle. The space had the same holiness, a weight that didn't feel heavy. The two leaders watched me as I took in the room. I couldn't find the words to articulate the gift of being back in the sanctuary that looked so different yet contained the same Spirit it had always held. Eventually, in part to assure them, I responded inadequately, "It's beautiful." I hope I didn't say anything as ridiculous as "I like what you've done with the place," but I surely could have given my stunned awe.

The beauty of the space was not just an aesthetic intention, but a theological one. Within Orthodox spaces, "Everything that surrounds you is supposed to evoke the Presence of God and make the invisible visible, the nontangible tangible. In the temple or church building design and in every aspect of its decoration, everything should be as beautiful as possible. Why? Because Beauty is a characteristic of God's Nature. We worship the Lord in the Beauty of Holiness, and God is the Creator and Source of all Beauty. God is beautiful! Heaven is beautiful! Being in God's Presence is beautiful! The Orthodox church building, the temple, makes the invisible divine realm and its beauty visible."[1]

A large egg-shaped silver bowl on a stand in the front of the sanctuary served as their baptismal font, where a child sits in the water. Fr. Thomas pointed out our tiny wooden font with a bowl at the back of the sanctuary. Even though they didn't have any use for our small font, they couldn't bear to get rid of it either. He understood the history and significance of that furnishing. In a quiet act of honoring people they never met and a community they never knew, the Basilios-Gregorios people kept St. Peter's font sitting inside the sanctuary, near the door. Mr. Jacob pointed out how the congregation kept not just the baptismal font, but also the altar table, table of gifts, and even the shelf that was hung on the back wall of the altar space. They understood their holiness, their preciousness, and kept them.

As we talked about the font, I heard the curtains opening and turned to face the front of the sanctuary, revealing the high altar. Covered in intricately detailed red and gold paraments, the altar table was the focal point of the whole space. Ascending shelves sat on it, which held tall gold candlesticks, and a large gold cross stood tall at the center. The space around the altar, left open with the removal of our old electric organ and speakers, only served to pull the focus back to the center of worship.

As we stood in the sanctuary, the men shared a bit about their lives, the story of St. Thomas in India, and the history of their church. We took pictures of our group. As I was about to leave, I talked about the stained-glass windows and how much the people of St. Peter's valued them. I mentioned that some people wanted to take them with us. The men looked shocked. They had checked out many places for their permanent church home. Some buildings had more parking or were closer to where most of their people lived, but the stained-glass windows of our little church kept persuading them to zero in on this precious space.

Fr. Thomas asked if I knew any stories about the people memorialized in the nameplates installed in the windows. Their people were curious

1. Sr. Ionna, "Orthodox Churches," para. 2.

about the people behind those names. We walked around the perimeter of the sanctuary as I introduced them to some of our people. We came to the David window that Grace gave, in "loving remembrance of Mother and Dad." Smiling at the memories of them, I told Father Thomas and Mr. Jacob how Grace had sung in the choir for decades, about her deep faith and compassion for all people, her almost naïve love, which assumed the best in people. Roy had been much like Mr. Jacob, taking good care of the property.

I led them out of the sanctuary to a large stained-glass window in the gathering space. It was the newest of all the windows, simple and modern, depicting a big cross surrounded by blocks of bright colored glass. "To the glory of God" was written boldly at the bottom. Roy and Grace gave that window with the same humility they lived, not to glorify themselves, or even to point to the goodness of the congregation they loved so deeply, but simply to the glory of God. The window now welcomed people into a space full of beauty and divinity, a room no one could walk into without glorifying God.

A friend once told me that the proof of God's existence can be found in a person whose life only makes sense because of the presence of God in them. God, in other words, is the only answer that could possibly explain how they could live as kindly as they do. Grace and Roy were such people. So were a host of other St. Peter's people whose names didn't make it onto windows, but who are permanently inscribed on my heart. Their lives of generosity and open-heartedness, delight and compassion, and ultimate self-giving were all a tribute to God.

My mind turned to the current congregation occupying this building. Grace had always dreamed that a new congregation would make a home within those walls. She prayed that it would remain a place where people worshiped God, that someday the Sunday School rooms would again be full of kids learning about Jesus, where people would come to know Christ, and where service and generosity would flourish. Through the faithfulness of the leaders of Saints Basilios-Gregorios Orthodox Church, that building continues to be what it has been for decades—a sanctuary, a community center, a place of learning and joy, where people live in ways that make no sense unless the Spirit is alive within them.

God proved faithful yet again. Not unlike Thomas, our doubts turned to confident trust. Yet again, the Spirit breathed new life into people and places. To the Glory of God.

24

2009-Now

Unlocking the Doors

[Jesus said,] "I will give you the keys of the kingdom of heaven, and whatever you bind on earth will be bound in heaven, and whatever you loose on earth will be loosed in heaven" (Matthew 16:19).

A few months after St. Peter's closed, our Bishop invited me to serve as an interim pastor at a congregation a few towns south of us in central New Jersey. Thanks to my severance, I had a few months of renewal without working, but I doubted myself and my abilities in pastoral leadership. I looked at other career opportunities and explored what else I could do with myself. Given my track record as a pastor, I wondered if I could be trusted with another congregation. But that invitation from our Bishop gave me a little confidence. Perhaps I wasn't so awful if I was being called off the bench.

So, I stepped back into the role as pastor and accompanied a congregation through the grief and new beginnings after their founding pastor left. In return, they ushered me through my own grief and new beginnings. They proved to be just the kind of community I needed to learn to trust myself again. It didn't take a lot. Just a community of open-hearted people who simply expected that I could do what they called me to do. That's the funny thing about confidence. It's often built by just doing the act that scares us and, in that effort, realizing we're capable.

The following summer, I received an email from a pastor of a congregation in Iowa looking for an associate pastor. I love small congregations and never imagined working at a big, multi-staff church. However, the position allowed me to focus on the aspects of ministry that I love. I would have brilliant, faithful colleagues with whom I could collaborate creatively, and a loving bunch of people to serve. The Spirit moves in surprising ways and carried me to a congregation that has been my home ever since, a community that has loved me back into myself.

It's amazing the capacity of a human heart to keep loving, even when it is broken. It just takes some tenderness, authentic belonging, and the security of being known. This is what I came to experience in loving community as I found my footing in Iowa. Jesus taught about being faithful with a little and faithful with much. I have been among the most privileged of pastors to have served a small congregation that was generous with just a little, and a large congregation that knows how to be generous with its many resources. Webs of connection and care can be woven wherever people of faith meet together, no matter the size of a place.

The healing that follows grief is strange and surprising. Often, it is only in looking back that we see the people God placed in our lives to help build us back together. In hindsight, we see the people whose presence, invitations, persistence, tenderness, and courage drew us out of ourselves and back into the world. Most of the time, the restoration we need comes from outside ourselves, from people who reach out and pull us forward. New life begins with someone knocking on our doors when we lock them securely, afraid and doubtful.

Dietrich Bonhoeffer describes this reality in a letter he wrote while being held in a Nazi prison. In November of 1943, he compared the ways we wait for healing and new life to being in a prison cell, where "one waits, hopes, and does this, or that, or the other, things that are really no consequence, but the door is shut, and can only be opened from the outside."[1] Often, our healing and freedom come from the outside. This has been true for me. My staff colleagues and congregants, with their invitations to friendship, to try creative ministry opportunities, to grow my abilities with honest feedback, and simply to be myself, gave me freedom and joy. It came from the outside.

This outside-in theology is evident in one of the stained-glass windows at St. Peter's. A reproduction of a painting by the English pre-Raphaelite

1. Bonhoeffer, *Letters and Papers from Prison,* 135.

artist William Holeman Hunt, "The Light of the World." The painting depicts Jesus knocking at a door in a garden. Hunt painted the original to illustrate the lines from Revelation 3:20, "Listen! I am standing at the door, knocking; if you hear my voice and open the door, I will come in and eat with you, and you with me." Similar paintings have been created, including the most common one in the United States, by Warner Sallman. "Knocking at Heart's Door" depicts a light-skinned Jesus with perfectly styled, wavy, light-brown hair, bathed in divine light, as he knocks at a door.

This image gained popularity among American evangelical Christians who believe that salvation depends on a person's ability to say the right words to accept Jesus as their personal Savior. If they don't speak the right words of invitation, maybe Jesus moves on to the next house. However, my Lutheran Christian theology teaches that salvation is given to us not by anything we do, but because of all that Jesus has already done. It's all a gift, given to us freely. The surprising and miraculous grace is that Jesus has been in our hearts all along. Jesus does not need to knock to get into a place he already calls home. He doesn't need an invitation with perfectly formed words. He never gives up on us if the house isn't clean. Jesus has simply been with us, for us, and in us from the beginning.

However, this painting does point to the truth Bonhoeffer named, which I experienced in the months after St. Peter's closed. The door can only be opened from the outside. I couldn't find the new life and healing I hoped for by myself. I needed the invitation, the encouragement, and the challenge of others who opened that door. Maybe, instead of seeing that stained-glass door-knocking Jesus as depicting a door to some cozy inner part of ourselves, it shows the locked door of whatever real or metaphorical prison holds us captive. Jesus knocks to break the door open. "Come out!" he says, like he did to Lazarus, dead in his tomb. The door opens from the outside. The rock has been rolled away. We are free. We can step out of whatever cage or chains contain us.

My fifth-grade son has a friend who regularly shows up at our door, ringing the doorbell repeatedly and impatiently. When I answer, this scrawny and often-shy kid asks, "Can Amos come over to my house to play?" Before I can answer, my son is putting on his shoes, excited for whatever adventure lies ahead.

The door-knocking Jesus invites us out to play, to serve, to step into the wild adventure of following him. He frees us from the ways our grief or shame hold us captive. Given his itinerant life, Jesus often invited himself into other people's homes. Just as frequently, maybe even more, he drew people out of themselves and their comfortable dwellings and ways of thinking. "Come, follow me. Drop your nets. Give away what holds you back. Let go. Get up and walk." This liberating work is at the heart of Jesus' ministry and who we, as his people, now get to be for one another. We can follow Jesus in knocking on doors and inviting people out to play.

I read somewhere from some grief expert (what does it mean to be a grief expert—are not so many of us?) that the task of grief is moving from what was to what is. Living forward through grief means taking stock of a new reality and living into what that means. The work of grief is opening the door when someone knocks and choosing to step out, even when staying inside feels comfortingly familiar. When someone we love dies, it means figuring out how to solve a problem without a Dad to call or how to handle taxes when your partner had always done them. When a congregation dies, it means figuring out where to worship, how to make new meaning, where to serve, and with whom we build community. This work is never a straight line but is messy and complicated.

For a long time, many people have believed that the stages of grief happen linearly, as if to check off a list of prescribed and universal feelings. These stages, first described by Elisabeth Kubler-Ross, are often considered a roadmap of when and what to feel. First, we feel denial, then anger, then bargaining, followed by depression, until we make our way to acceptance. However, this common understanding was never Kubler-Ross's intention, and it doesn't accurately represent my own experience of grief or what I've observed in others. She names some of the feelings that people feel after a loss, but we seldom go through them in such a straightforward way. Grief is not a to-do list of feelings any more than faith is uttering a simple phrase that welcomes Jesus into our hearts.

Instead, grief is more of a dance between two modes of being, as Margaret Stroebe and Henk Schut call it, the "Dual Process Model."[2] We process death and loss through two modes, loss-oriented ways of being and restoration-oriented ones. The loss-oriented actions include rituals around death, telling the stories, remembering, and feeling all the unexpected sadnesses that arrive unannounced. Restoration-oriented ways include activities like getting back to work, to life, and investing in new beginnings. We oscillate between these two modes. We are primarily in a loss-oriented mode soon after a loss, but over time, we spend more time in a restoration-oriented

2. Stroebe and Schut, "Dual Process Model."

way of being. But never wholly; there are seasons or moments when we are pulled back into the depth of the pain of loss, sometimes even years later.

We oscillate between loss and restoration. It happened for me and those in my community over the years since our closing. The paths forward were never straight or direct but were rather messy, circuitous, and complicated; for many of us, they continue. As I look back, I can see that so much of my own restoration came from the outside, from people who kept knocking on my door to invite me out of my fear and shame. When I drew the shades and locked the deadbolt, they busted down the door. In hindsight, I see they embodied Jesus and his door-knocking ways, pulling me toward restoration and healing when I couldn't see it myself.

Whenever artists depict St. Peter in stained glass, icons, or paintings, they show him carrying a set of keys. This identifying symbol comes from Jesus giving Simon the name Peter (*petros,* rock): "I will give you the keys of the kingdom of heaven, and whatever you bind on earth will be bound in heaven, and whatever you loose on earth will be loosed in heaven" (Matt.16:19). For centuries this has been understood to mean that Peter, and the leaders in the church who follow in his footsteps, have the power to forgive sin.

However, the Ministry of the Keys is more than just assigning a few "Hail Marys" to someone after they confess some inappropriate thoughts. The church is about breaking the chains of all that goes against God and God's great dream of life and love for this world. We are all held captive by actions that hurt and harm, by systems of the world that limit and oppress, by fear, by privilege, by addictions, by prejudice, by grief, and so much more. We cannot unlock ourselves; what liberates us is Jesus and his life-giving grace; this is the power of the keys.

While some traditions hold that only a few designated leaders can carry these keys of loosening or opening up new life, I've experienced God handing out keys to everyday people. It's like when everyone at St. Peter's seemed to have a master key to the main door of that brick church, whether it was given to them by Roy or someone else. It's like the Persian poet Hafiz wrote:

> The small man
> Builds cages for everyone
> He
> Knows.
> While the sage,
> Who has to duck his head
> When the moon is low,

Keeps dropping keys all night long
For the
Beautiful
Rowdy
Prisoners.[3]

Many sages dropped keys for me throughout the months and years after St. Peter's closed. The most important ones were those who helped me regain my footing and trust that God had indeed called me to be a pastor. Some of those were big things, like an invitation to begin a new call and serve as a pastor, an acknowledgement of my gifts. But most were smaller—an email naming that a sermon seemed to speak grace right to their own situation, a kid wrapping their arms around my legs while I served communion, an opportunity to contribute to a writing project, or a quiet smile of recognition and welcome from a parishioner in their hospice bed.

In these last years, I received the keys, both literal and figurative ones, to St. Paul Lutheran Church, a congregation that by some grace, has allowed me to be authentically myself as their pastor, in all my quirks and gifts and failures. And, while we are much more restrained with the actual keys we give out, it's my prayer that everyone who steps into the doors of our congregation will experience that same acceptance and celebration of who they are, and a place to use those gifts for the good of others.

When we are locked in the cages of our grief, bound up by guilt, or diminished by a sense of failure, God sends us people who knock on our door with one aim in mind: to unbind us as graciously as possible. Some dear women gave me those keys while eating at a diner in New Jersey, walking along the Jersey shore, talking in the company of cacti in Arizona. In hearing their experiences of being liberated and finding new life, they offered forgiveness and freedom for me. The re-storying of our experience together restored me.

Over and over again, in the years since St. Peter's closed, I've been gifted by people who have dropped keys in my lap. "Come out and play," they've said, "Come and serve here. Join us as we embark on this adventure of faith. You don't have to be perfect, just be you. You, beautiful and rowdy, you are just who we need."

3. Hafiz, "Dropping Keys," 206.

Conclusion

Then one of the elders addressed me, saying, "Who are these, robed in white, and where have they come from?" I said to him, "Sir, you are the one who knows." Then he said to me, "These are they who have come out of the great ordeal; they have washed their robes and made them white in the blood of the Lamb" (Revelation 7:13–14).

WHILE THE SPECIFIC STORIES found in this book are particular to me and the people of St. Peter's, our reality is not unique. Countless congregations in my denomination and throughout the United States are navigating similar waters. They are running low on resources and are desperately wondering how to honor their past while being honest about their future. They are trying to figure out how to keep serving their neighbor despite increasingly limited capacity. They are asking themselves, "Given this reality, how can we be faithful?"

I hope that this story can bring some courage and companionship to others, and a vision of what might be possible on the other side of loss. I decided to write this eulogy for people who consistently and persistently showed me what faith, generosity, and courage look like. On the other side of this challenging and painful experience of closing a church, I came to a few insights. Perhaps these convictions can assist others as they navigate a challenging time of being the church in North America today.

CONGREGATIONS MATTER

When religious skeptics hear of a church closing, they often point to this as proof that the Church is a failed experiment, never intended by God to succeed. They notice the pain and assume it's evidence of the brokenness of the whole enterprise, the demise of the whole institutional church. The opposite is true, however. The pain that comes from closing a church only demonstrates the importance of congregations.

We would not mourn something we did not love. The fact that "my" people still weep more than a decade after our church's closing only underscores how much congregations matter. The time and energy we invest in forming communities of belonging is worthwhile. Shaping worship that transforms matters. Creating avenues for building compassion, justice, and joy has tremendous value. If it didn't, none of this would hurt as much, and none of us would have been so fiercely committed to one another through all our differences.

Glennon Doyle has unforgettable insights about grief and love in her book, *Love Warrior*: "Grief is love's souvenir. It's our proof that we once loved. Grief is the receipt we wave in the air that says to the world, 'Look!' Love was once mine. I loved well. Here is my proof that I paid the price."[1]

Initially, after St. Peter's closed, the thought of loving another community of faith and being loved by them, of immersing myself in their beautiful and complicated goodness, felt terrifying and impossible. But the more I processed my grief, the more I came to know that my pain pointed not to the wrongness of parish life but to its necessity.

So, too, it was for so many of our people. They, too, waved the receipt of love from a life invested in a congregation of faith. For many of them, it was keys in the hands of others who opened doors of leadership and participation that drew them in. The openness of St. Peter's people to invest in a new community of God's people cannot be understated. Stepping out to love again after being heartbroken is no easy feat. But the Spirit of God promises to move, and does, and Jesus gets pushy. As I learned firsthand, God is a persistent God when it comes to pursuing our restoration and freedom.

CHURCH WITH A CAPITAL C

The Church is much larger than individual congregations. Even if congregations end their ministry, communities of faithful people will always be telling the stories of Jesus, sharing bread and wine, and caring for their neighbors. Congregations, as an entity within Christ's Church, may never have been intended to live on or exist forever. The church in Corinth and

1. Doyle, *Love Warrior*, 205.

those begun by St. Thomas in Kerala centuries ago are no longer. But their message, their witness, lives on. We may push hard against the notion that everything has a life cycle, but life cycles are nonetheless real. If we forget this, the prophet Isaiah will certainly remind us. "The grass withers, the flowers fade, but the word of our God will stand forever."

The word of God stands forever. While we humans and our human institutions are like grass, God's word will not die. And God's people, the Church, will not either. Even though St. Peter's died, in a very real sense, our people, the building, and resources continue to live on, expressing the Gospel in all kinds of new places and creative ways. Christians are always part of something much bigger than they can conceive or imagine, and certainly bigger than our own individual congregations or even denominations represent. This awareness is vital to keep in mind, as it provides the courage and hope needed when the decline or death of our institutions becomes a reality.

In the fall of 2025, I sat under the heat of the early summer sun with several thousand Tanzanian Lutherans at the 50th celebration of the Pare Diocese of the Evangelical Lutheran Church of Tanzania. We sang a song I learned forty years earlier in the basement of Valley Lutheran Church in Westminster, Colorado. "Asante Sana Jesu," we sang, "asante sana Jesu. Asante sana Jesu moyomi." The people of Valley Lutheran taught us to sing "Thank you, Jesus" in Swahili in Sunday School. I'm sure we mispronounced the words, but we experienced in our voices that the Church is so much bigger than just our congregation, comprised of communities who speak many languages, on continents on the other side of the world.

I hadn't sung that song for years, until standing on the red dirt of northern Tanzania, bearing witness to the ways the Lutheran Christian Church flourished, transforming the spirits and bodies of people throughout the region. Our family had spent the week with a little village in the mountains called Kirangare, where a small parish of Lutherans demonstrated their faith and generosity with ginger tea, enormous meals, and extravagant worship. The leaders of the parish showed us how they served the community through sewing machines, a deep freezer at a dairy store, and the preschool for the most vulnerable children. The little Colorado church that taught me how to sing "Asante sana Jesu" no longer exists, but the Church is vibrantly alive in Tanzania and throughout the world.

A broader ecclesiology not only brings us radical hope and deeper solidarity with people around the world, but also helps us to let go of what we cling to. Trusting that our congregations or even our denominations are not singular can free us and our resources. Knowing that the church does not exist for itself but for the world ought to unlock the treasure chests of joyous generosity. Seeing ourselves in unity with other followers of Jesus is ample motivation for investing in creative ministries, compassion-building and justice-making organizations, and communities that historically have been under-resourced. The sturdier our faith grows, the easier it becomes to let loose the resources that we otherwise tend to hold protectively.

In February 2025, shortly after baseless rumors spread nationally that Lutheran Social Services, a ministry arm of our church that responds to people in great need, had laundered money and stolen from the government, the presiding bishop of the ELCA responded with a statement. Bishop Elizabeth Eaton said, "In the year 258, the Roman Empire, during one of its many persecutions of the church, ordered that the church turn over its treasure. The task fell to a young deacon named Lawrence, who was given three days to complete it. Immediately, Lawrence sold all the liquid assets and gave them to the sick and to the widows. He also liquidated all of the property and divided that up amongst the poor. On the third day, he appeared before the emperor, who demanded to see the treasures of the church. Lawrence gestured behind him, and there were standing those who were sick and hungry, the poor, the naked, the stranger in the land, the most vulnerable, and Lawrence said, 'These are the treasures of the church.' He was martyred for that. Be of good courage, Church, and let us persevere."[2]

Jesus invites us to the freedom found in following Lawrence, giving ourselves away, and realizing that the treasures of our church are always found in people. Our courage comes when we remember that we are not singular but bound up in a community, a tradition, a faith, that is so much bigger than ourselves.

CHANGING THE NARRATIVE OF FAILURE

Over a decade after St. Peter's closed, I sat in a hotel ballroom at an assembly of Lutherans from throughout southeastern Iowa. Although necessary for the order of the church, these meetings are not widely known for being stimulating. But I was unprepared for the wave of grief and gratitude I would experience that evening. Just after we celebrated ordination and congregational anniversaries, the tone of the evening shifted sharply. Two

2 Eaton, "ELCA Responds," 01:52–02:25.

congregations in our synod held services of "Holy Closure," as it was called, their ending.

The bishop used some of her time at the podium to share stories of these congregations' ministries, display photographs of their buildings, and show snapshots of their people. As she spoke about the difference they made in their neighborhoods and the world, she delivered their eulogies. But lest any of the conference participants presumed the beauty of these congregations was gone, members present from those communities were asked to stand. The whole assembly applauded vigorously. We put our hands together to say, "Well done, good and faithful servants." Then, our Bishop prayed for them with gratitude for their years of ministry, just as she blessed them for their next chapters. I sat with my half-eaten hotel cheesecake in front of me, tears streaming down my face. I had never before experienced this sort of public honoring of a church that had ended, a communal naming of the loss for the whole church, combined with a celebration of their faithfulness.

The narrative about church endings needs to be reframed or perhaps scrapped for stories that are not only more life-giving but also more true. As more congregations close, we must create rituals to celebrate their ministry and faithfulness, even as we mourn their closure. Doing this would honor the vast array of losses that members of these communities experience, while also alleviating the shame or guilt that many of them carry.

In his book, *When God Speaks Through Worship,* Craig Satterlee writes about a congregation he served that faithfully chose to close. He wrote:

> The members of St. Timothy's Church were faithful, courageous people who chose to take seriously what it means to deny themselves, to take up their cross, and to lose their lives for the sake of Jesus and the gospel. They knew and trusted the proclamation of Christ crucified as the power and the wisdom of God that brings life out of death. Many people outside the congregation appreciated what St. Timothy's Church did on that day as the gospel proclamation we intended, but not everyone. Some, both inside and outside our church, could only see closing as a failure, foolishness, a stumbling block.[3]

Too often, we hear the message that a church closing is a sign of failure and faithlessness. But the stories of St. Peter's, St. Timothy's, and so many other congregations show that the end of a congregation is actually a move

3. Satterlee, *When God Speaks,* 121–122.

of courageous faith, of people who choose to lose their lives for the sake of others.

BOLD NEW STORIES

These are not easy times for the Church. The realities of dwindling numbers, increasing debt, and declining churches can weigh heavily on leaders, fostering a range of despair. But if we pause long enough to think about it, God has given us exactly what we need to face these days with honest hope: stories. These stories are not only found in Scripture but are often more vividly portrayed in the lives of the very people who inhabit our pews.

The stories we tell matter. "Fairy tales are more than true—not because they tell us that dragons exist, but because they tell us that dragons can be beaten,"[4] wrote G.K. Chesterton. Dragons and the challenges they present are not hard to see. But we also need stories about how those dragons can be conquered. To live with courageous hope in these times doesn't require that we retell the story of St. George killing the dragon. We just have to be perceptive enough to spot a small group of people giving away their treasures for the sake of an unknown future, and of a church that will look different from what we are now but will still be a witness to Jesus and his transforming love in this world. We know the dragons are real, but we also need to know that they will not win.

I don't know what every one of those stories will be, but they will not be stories of mega-churches, unstoppable growth, shiny faith, or some cozy alignment with an empire's power. They certainly won't glamorize prosperity, ease, or privilege. Rather, they will be stories of self-giving and allegiance to the poor, of love for the outcast that persists and perseveres, and of a church that clings to Jesus above all else.

Brian McLaren names the importance of finding new stories, or reclaiming and remembering old, liberating ones. He makes a point of noting that our institutions were framed within "social narratives or framing stories that are failing us . . . fantasies of unlimited growth, wish-dreams about guaranteed happy endings, delusions of power, fables of inevitable progress. But, I remind myself, our humanity cannot be reduced to our current narratives and institutions. As they fail, we can disentangle and step away from them. We can tell better, more honest, more healing stories, and we can build better, wiser, more durable, representative, and ethical institutions,

4 Quoted in Evans, *Inspired*, xxi.

starting small, and, if necessary, rebuilding the ruins or replanting the ashes . . . Could we discover, tell, and live a new story, a love story of renaissance, resilience, and even resurrection?"[5]

What stories might we tell about people living with courageous love, sharing the story of Jesus, and giving their treasures away so that others might live? How do we imagine a new future for the people of God that is unencumbered by idolatry to what we always were, and imagine how we might become for the thriving of humanity and sustaining of the whole creation? Perhaps these days of endings and decline might be our opportunity as followers of Jesus to take his stories of yeast and mustard seeds, cross-bearing, and self-giving seriously. Our hope might just be in those stories, in our ancient prayers, and in new practices, stories, and liturgies that emerge.

TRUSTING IN RESURRECTION

We can imagine new futures, change the narratives of our endings, because as Christians, all of our stories find their source in Jesus, the resurrected one. At the heart of our faith is this trust that even as things end, somehow, through God's grace, they are not dead. We need this foundational story, especially as we come face-to-face with endings.

In February of 2025, the congregation in Colorado that began as St. Peter's ended, The House for All Saints and Sinners, held its final service. When I heard this news, I felt sadness for a community within which I had never worshipped, but who so beautifully reclaimed and reused not only the brass candlesticks from St. Peter's but also the practices of our Lutheran tradition. I mourned the loss of a community that bore witness to God's gracious embrace of people who didn't always experience it. A few months later, their founding pastor, Nadia Bolz-Weber wrote about this ending of the congregation she served and still loves.

> We may grieve something or someone who *was* here and now *is not*, but the people and times and events of our lives that are now "gone," just sort of live in diaspora in the world.
>
> Because maybe the physics of love defies the binary gravity of grief . . .
>
> Maybe all the love, creativity, hilarity, solace, and tenderness that we've ever known—every belly laugh, every whispered secret,

5. McLaren, *Life After Doom*, 225–226.

> every late-night road trip with bad gas-station coffee, every hand we've ever held in both joy and grief—maybe all of that is not actually gone.
>
> Maybe it ends up forming the connective tissue in our lives, invisible but strong, like the ligaments that keep our bones from flying apart . . .
>
> So if you're still standing, it might not be because you're strong. It might be because you are held together by the love you've received and maybe even the love you gave, whether or not you knew what the hell you were doing at the time.
>
> Maybe that's what resurrection looks like; the people we mourn, the physics of their love is ineffable. It's not dispelled—it's dispersed. Micronized. Reconfiguring. But never actually GONE.[6]

This witness to the mystery of resurrection names the ways I am held, have been held. The people of St. Peter's remain as ligaments for me, connective tissue holding my bones together. They are not gone, just reconfigured. The same is true for all those dear ones who remain present to me, micronized by the power of the resurrection, even though they have died. But none more than my Dad.

A few days after we brought my Dad home for hospice care, our family and closest friends filled every seat in our living room to sing a beautiful liturgy known as Holden Evening Prayer. This simple setting of the ancient liturgy for the close of the day had been a part of the rhythm of our lives since I was a child. We ended dinners with friends or holiday celebrations in those sung prayers, grounding our lives in the promise of Christ, "the light of the world, the light no darkness can overcome" (John 1:1). So, in Dad's last days, with our house full of friends and the shadow of death surrounding us, singing together the hope of our faith seemed the right thing to do. It didn't just *seem* the right thing to do; it *was* the right thing to do.

When the time came for the scripture reading, my dying Dad cleared his throat. With his voice as strong as his body was weak, he said, "A reading from Revelation." He proceeded to recite, from heart, the words of scripture that would be read at church the coming Sunday, All Saints' Day. "After this, I looked, and there was a great multitude that no one could count, from every nation, from all tribes and peoples and languages, standing before the throne and before the Lamb, robed in white, with palm branches in their hands. They cried out in a loud voice, saying, "Salvation belongs to our God who is seated on the throne and to the Lamb!" . . . Then

6. Bolz-Weber, *The Lesbian Whisperer.*

one of the elders addressed me, saying, "Who are these, robed in white, and where have they come from?" I said to him, "Sir, you are the one who knows." Then he said to me, "These are they who have come out of the great ordeal; they have washed their robes and made them white in the blood of the Lamb" (Rev. 7: 9–10, 13–14).

Silence filled the room like the weight of a wool blanket. The comfort and hope in this ancient-future story embraced us. After he caught his breath, Dad began to preach one last time. He told a story about those faithful who had endured the great ordeal. He spoke about how they had suffered terribly before God carried them to healing and restoration. Dad named their struggles, the heartbreak and grief they endured. He shared his own ordeals, the pain of these last months, the sorrow of saying goodbye. But then Dad described *how* those robes were washed clean. It wasn't with laundry soap and washing machines. They were washed with tears. Their sorrow brought them hope. By the power of the blood of the Lamb, the suffering and resurrection of our Savior, their tears were not the end, but the means by which they found redemption.

In the story of robes being washed clean with tears, of those who had been through the great ordeal, Dad connected our story to the great, ancient, and eternal story of God's restoration of the whole cosmos. Our sorrows were not isolated in that living room. Our struggle was not the end of the story. Our tears were not wasted, but used for our healing. We were part of a great long line of people who have loved and lost, not gone, but dispersed. People who grieve and despair, and who are gathered up by Christ's death and resurrection and given new life. Death and life, dying and rising, endings and beginnings, crucifixion and resurrection.

In what has become known as the Beatitudes, Jesus said, "Blessed are those who mourn, for they will be comforted" (Matt. 5:4). Jesus names the reality that we will weep, mourn, and grieve in this life. And, in the same sentence, he names the promise that joy constitutes the other side of weeping. Surely, this peasant faithful man knew the Psalms up and down, including Psalm 30, "Weeping may endure through the night, but joy comes in the morning." For a long time, I thought the last word of that verse was not morning, as in the beginning of the day, but mourning, as in the work of grief. But perhaps both are true. Joy takes time, a few sleep cycles of the sun. But joy also comes in mourning, in making space to grieve and name all that was lost and all that we have suffered to wash our robes clean with our tears. God carries us, and in the morning, in the mourning, we will find joy.

This is the paschal mystery, the great mystery that is intertwined with every story of human significance. "Christ has died. Christ is risen. Christ will come again." Or, to put it differently, we can trust that Christ will bring a new beginning to every ending. This is true for us in our own death, and it is true for our congregations in their own closures and endings, too. Joy comes in the mourning. Joy comes in the morning. Even though we die, we live.

Bibliography

Bolz-Weber, Nadia. "The Lesbian Whisperer: on Chocolate, Loss, Buttons and." *The Corners*, September 7, 2025. https://thecorners.substack.com/p/the-diaspora-of-love.

Bonhoeffer, Dietrich. *Letters and Papers from Prison.* New York: Macmillan, 1973.

Boorstein, Michelle. "Bolz-Weber's Liberal, Foulmouthed Articulation of Christianity Speaks to Fed-up Believers," *Washington Post*, November 3, 2013.

Brueggemann, Walter. *Spirituality of the Psalms.* Minneapolis: Augsburg Fortress, 2002.

Churchill, Winston. "House of Commons Rebuilding." Speech, London, October 28, 1943. House of Commons Hansard. https://api.parliament.uk/historic-hansard/commons/1943/oct/28/house-of-commons-rebuilding.

Cumming, Richard. "End Hunger? The Single Most Important Step." ELCA World Hunger (blog). Evangelical Lutheran Church in America, July 25, 2016. https://blogs.elca.org/worldhunger/end-hunger-single-important-step/.

Dinesen, Isak. *Seven Gothic Tales.* New York: Vintage, 1991.

Donne, John. "No Man Is an Island." In *Devotions Upon Emergent Occasions, 1624.* Project Gutenberg, 2007. http://www.gutenberg.org/files/19685/19685-h/19685-h.htm.

Doyle, Glennon. *Love Warrior.* New York: Flatiron, 2016.

Dueuck, Jason. "Palestinian Christian Leaders Ask for Compassion, Prayer and Action," *Anabaptist World.* December 22, 2023. https://anabaptistworld.org/palestinian-christian-leaders-ask-for-compassion-prayer-and-action/

Eaton, Elizabeth. "ELCA Responds to False Accusations on X 02-02-2025." Evangelical Lutheran Church in America, posted February 2, 2025. YouTube, 2:42. https://www.youtube.com/watch?v=LiqzoVdZG1E

Erasmus, Desiderius, and Charles Trinkaus. *Collected Works of Erasmus: Controversies, Volume 76.* Toronto: University of Toronto Press, 1999. https://research.ebsco.com/linkprocessor/plink?id=acd9515e-bfd3-3d7c-a1be-0ec1e5563647.

Evangelical Lutheran Church in America. "ELCA World Hunger: DIKO Marie's Story (Niem, Central African Republic)" posted November 21, 2012. YouTube, 6:18. https://www.youtube.com/watch?v=JjoshQtQxgY

———. *Evangelical Lutheran Worship.* Minneapolis: Augsburg Fortress, 2006.

———. *Evangelical Lutheran Worship Leader's Ritual Edition.* Minneapolis: Augsburg Fortress, 2006.

Evans, Rachel Held. *Inspired: Slaying Giants, Walking on Water, and Loving the Bible Again.* Nashville: Nelson, 2018.

Gillman, Bob. "Bind Us Together" In *With One Voice: A Lutheran Resource for Worship.* Minneapolis: Augsburg Fortress, 1995.

Hafiz. "Dropping Keys." In *The Gift: Poems Inspired by Hafiz, the Great Sufi Master.* Rendered by Daniel Ladinsky. New York: Penguin Compass, 1999.

Halverson, Chris. "Evelyn Troy Funeral Sermon," Sermon, St. Stephen's Lutheran Church, October 3, 2013.

Halverson, Chris, and Linda Nietman, *"Seeing with the Mind. Hearing with the Heart: A Thematic Bible Study on the Gospel of Luke by a Young Pastor and a Not So Young Parishioner."* Xulon, 2015.

Heat-Moon, William Least. *River Horse.* New York: Penguin, 1999.

How, William W. "For All the Saints." In *Evangelical Lutheran Worship*, no. 422. Minneapolis: Augsburg Fortress, 2006.

Lathrop, Gordon. *Holy Things: A Liturgical Theology.* Minneapolis: Augsburg Fortress, 1993.

Levine, Sam. "ICE Could add 600 beds to New Jersey Detention Center, Documents Show." *The Guardian,* November 22, 2024. https://www.theguardian.com/us-news/2024/nov/22/ice-new-jersey-detention.

Lewis, Alan E. *Between Cross and Resurrection: A Theology of Holy Saturday.* Grand Rapids: Eerdmans, 2001.

Lischer, Richard. "Stripped Bare, Holy Week and the Art of Losing." *Christian Century,* March 21, 2012, 11–12.

Luther, Martin. *Luther's Works, Vol. 5: Lectures on Genesis Chapters* 26–30. Edited by Jaroslav Pelikan. Translated by George V. Schick. St. Louis: Concordia Publishing House, 1968.

Lutheran Church in America. *Lutheran Book of Worship.* Minneapolis: Augsburg, 1978.

Lutkin, Peter C. "*The Lord Bless You and Keep You.*" In Chalice Hymnal, edited by the Chalice Hymnal Committee, no. 446. St. Louis: Chalice, 1995.

Katz, Matt. "ICE Jailer in New Jersey is Sued by its Landlord, Claiming Unsafe Conditions." *Gothamist*, May 3, 2021. https://gothamist.com/news/ice-jailer-new-jersey-sued-its-landlord-claiming-unsafe-conditions.

Marsh, Donald Stuart, and Richard Kinsey Avery. "I am the church! You are the church!" Hope, 1972.

Martin, Civilla D. and Charles H. Gabriel, "His Eye Is on the Sparrow," In *Revival Hymns,* ed. Daniel B. Towner and Charles H. Gabriel. Chicago: Fleming H. Revell, 1905.

McLaren, Brian D. *Life After Doom: Wisdom and Courage for a World Falling Apart.* New York: St. Martin's Essentials, 2024.

Morgan, Alice. *What is Narrative Therapy? An Easy to Read Introduction.* Adelaide: Dulwich Centre, 2000.

Mortimer, John. *The Anti-social Behaviour of Horace Rumpole.* London: Viking, 2007.

New Jersey Synod, Evangelical Lutheran Church in America. *Celebration of Ministry and Closing of a Congregation,* 2009.

Oliver, Mary. "The Poet Thinks about the Donkey." In *Thirst.* Boston: Beacon, 2006.

Olson, Mark A. *The Evangelical Pastor.* Minneapolis: Augsburg Fortress, 1992.

———. *Notes to Eli.* Minneapolis: Kirkhouse, 2005.

Peterson, Eugene H. *Five Smooth Stones for Pastoral Work.* New York: Eerdmans, 1980.

———. *The Message: The Bible in Contemporary Language.* Colorado Springs: NavPress, 2002.

Rosen, Michael. *We're Going on a Bear Hunt.* New York: Little Simon, 1989.

Satterlee, Craig. *When God Speaks Through Worship: Stories Congregations Live By.* Herndon, VA: Alban Institute, 2009.

Sittler, Joseph. *The Ecology of Faith.* Philadelphia: Fortress, 1961.

Sr. Ionna, *"Why Orthodox Churches Look the Way They Do"* St. Innocent of Alaska Orthodox Monastery. Accessed September 28, 2025. https://stinnocentmonastery.org/whatintheworld_volume2.

Stroebe, Margaret, and Henk Schut. "The Dual Process Model of Coping with Bereavement: Rationale and Description." *Death Studies*, 23(3), October, 1999. https://doi.org/10.1080/074811899201046

Wambach, Abby, Glennon Doyle, and Amanda Doyle, hosts. *We Can Do Hard Things*, podcast, episode 340, "How Abby Survived Her Biggest Loss," August 27, 2024.

Welles, Orson, and Kodar, Oja. *The Big Brass Ring*. Edited by James Pepper and Jonathan Rosenbaum. Santa Barbara, California: Santa Teresa, 1987.

www.ingramcontent.com/pod-product-compliance
Lightning Source LLC
LaVergne TN
LVHW050640100826
845148LV00011B/1924

* 9 7 9 8 3 8 5 2 2 8 4 8 5 *